*JUDGMENT HAS BEGUN AND
REVIVAL IS KNOCKING AT THE DOORS!*

STORMY
WEATHER

AUTHOR OF *THE IDENTITY THEFT*
DOMINIQUAE
BIERMAN

STORMY WEATHER © 2005-2021 by Dominiquae Bierman

All rights reserved. This book may not be copied or reprinted for commercial gain or profit. The use of short quotations or occasional page copying for personal or group study is permitted and encouraged. Permission will be granted upon request.

Unless otherwise identified, Scripture quotations are from: *The King James Version* or *New American Standard Bible*. Used by permission. All rights reserved.

Published by *Zion's Gospel Press*

52 Tuscan Way, Ste 202-412
St. Augustine, FL, 32092
shalom@zionsgospel.com

Paperback ISBN: 978-1-953502-45-2
E-Book ISBN: 978-1-953502-46-9

On occasion words such as Jesus, Christ, Lord and God have been changed by the author, back to their original Hebrew renderings, Yeshua, Messiah, Yahveh, and ELOHIM.

Bold or italicized emphasis or underlining within quotations is the author's own.

Printed in the United States of America

First Printing December 2005, Second Printing June 2021

Dedication

This book is dedicated to all of my disciples and spiritual children worldwide.

Thanksgiving

To the Almighty for sending us Yeshua, His son, to rescue us from the judgment to come and to my Kad-Esh MAP team in Israel; Rabbi Baruch, my husband and number one supporter, my precious assistant and intercessor Rev. Daniel Flueckiger, who worked day and night researching data for this book. You are a faithful servant and a true warrior! To Karen, Jacki and Kim, a million thanks for proofreading and layout. Thank you for your prayers, love, support and practical help. I also want to thank Pastor David Yonggi Cho for establishing the Prayer Mountain in Korea, from where I have written this book.

Prophetic Word

The prophetic word that the Almighty gave me as I was praying for this book was in one of the prayer grottos of Prayer Mountain in South Korea, where I also wrote this book. I asked the Almighty to help me pray for Israel since I was crying out for the nations with all my heart, and He said:

> "I have Israel under the shadow of My wings but I am standing at the door of the nations with great anger and fury. My judgment is knocking at the door of every nation and yet My church is not ready, neither can it stand in the gap because of the lack of fear of God, lack of holiness and righteousness. So, I brought you here to cry out for the nations that are trying to destroy My inheritance Israel, and for the lukewarm and deceived church that has no power or substance to stand on at this time of stormy weather. This book has been given to you by Me, as a sign of

My great mercy to the nations and to My church. As many as I love, I warn, that they may repent"

Received on the 27th November 2005, 3:45 PM, Prayer Mountain - South Korea, Prayer Grotto number 25

The Judgment of the Nations

The great preacher, Charles Spurgeon, preached a message on "The Judgment of the Nations" on July 12, 1885. Excerpts of Spurgeon's message follow:

> There is a judgment also passing upon nations. For as nations will not exist as nations in another world, they have to be judged and punished in this present state. The thoughtful reader of history will not fail to observe how sternly this justice had dealt with empire after empire when they had become corrupt. Colossal dominions have withered to the ground when sentenced by the king of kings. Go and ask today, "Where is the empire of Assyria? Where are the mighty cities of Babylon? Where are the glories of the Medes and Persians? What has become of the Macedonian power? Where are the Caesars and their palaces?"
>
> The omnipotent judge has not ceased from His sovereign rule over Kingdoms, and our own country may yet have to feel His chastisements.

What is there about London [or the United States] that it should be more enduring than Rome? What are we? What is there about our boastful race, whether on this side of the Atlantic or the other, that we should monopolize the favor of God? If we rebel and sin against Him, He will not hold us guiltless but will deal out impartial justice to an ungrateful race. (Charles Spurgeon, *Judgment of the Nations, July 12, 1885)*

Terminology

I would like you to be familiar with some renewed terminology that will help your understanding. In any new move of God, there is new, or renewed terminology introduced. It is no different in the case of this End time move of restoration. Here are four terms which are used throughout the entire book. I would like you to be familiar with:

Yahveh

Yahveh is the name of the Lord as revealed to Moses and used throughout the prophetic writings. *Yahveh* means the "I AM" and the "Ever-Present God."

This name is often used in conjunction with the name; *Elohim*, which is the name of the "Creator God."

Yahveh Elohim

The I AM who is the Creator. The short way of saying Yahveh is Yah as in Halelu-Yah. So, many times I will use the Word Yah instead of "God."

The Torah

Torah is the Hebrew word for "instruction in righteousness," commonly called Law.

In this book, Torah only refers to the Law of Yahveh in the Five Books of Moses and Law throughout the Bible. In this book, the Torah does not apply to rabbinical laws or manmade traditions. In a place where I mention a rabbinical tradition, I will refer to it as such.

The Torah includes three types of charges:

- Commandments
- Statutes or Judgments
- Laws or Precepts

Because that Abraham obeyed My voice, and kept My charge, My commandments, My statutes, and My laws.

—Genesis 26:5

Notice that before Moses was given the Torah at Mount Sinai, Abraham already walked and obeyed the Torah. Abraham already followed the Torah since the Torah of the Living YAH (God) is eternal.

Notice that before Moses was given the Torah at Mount Sinai, Abraham already walked and obeyed the Torah. Abraham already followed the Torah since the Torah of the Living Yah (God) is eternal.

- The Commandments are eternal (referring to the Ten Commandments).
- The Statutes are also eternal and connected with holiness and worship. Note: following the Statutes connected with Temple Worship requires more background knowledge. Since we are now the Temple of the Holy Spirit, an interpretation from the Holy Spirit is needed about how to follow them today.
- The precepts are eternal principles, though the actual instructions were temporary and only relevant to the issues of the times they were given. So, today, we keep the principles and apply them to our times. As we walk with the Holy Spirit of Yah, He continues to give us precepts daily!

Here is the ticket to lifelong success and prosperity:

> This Book of the Law (Torah) shall not depart from your mouth, but you shall meditate in it day and night, that you may observe to do according to all that is written in it. For then you will make your way prosperous, and then you will have good success.
> —Joshua 1:8

Abraham, who is the father of the faith, understood and walked in the way which he had been given. Also in these End times, the Torah is being restored: a revelation by the Holy Spirit to the church. As we meditate in Yah's holy Commandments, judgments and precepts; the Word will become flesh in us and will produce the fruit of obedience. This obedience will make us blessed, successful, and prosperous.

Yeshua

Yeshua (commonly called Jesus Christ) is the real Hebrew name for the Jewish Messiah. In Hebrew, Yeshua means "salvation, deliverance and redemption." Throughout this book, I will use His Hebrew name only.

Yeshua is the Torah made flesh or the Living Torah. As you follow Him, and His *Ruach HaKodesh* (Holy Spirit) He will lead you to the Truth.

> And you shall know the truth, and the truth shall make you *free*.
>
> —John 8:32

Table of Contents

Chapter 1: Stormy Weather 3
Chapter 2: The Cause of Zion 17
Chapter 3: Gaza and Katrina. 27
Chapter 4: Weapons of Mass Destruction 55
Chapter 5: The Man That Stills the Storms. 85
Chapter 6: Are There Angels in the Storms? 97
Chapter 7: The Dynamics of Judgment. 123
Chapter 8: Repentance & Restitution 145
Chapter 9: Coming to the Original Foundations 157
Chapter 10: The Gospel of Obedience. 165
Chapter 11: A Church Like Esther 179
Chapter 12: True Leadership for Stormy Weather 197
Closure: Half an Hour of Prayer & Silence 209
Appendix A: Current Events 215
Appendix B: A Recount on Replacement Theology . .227
Appendix C: Revocation of the Council of Nicaea . . .231
Appendix D: Connect With Us. 241

FOREWORD

"Praise Yahveh from the earth, you great sea creatures, and all depths! Lightning and hail, snow and clouds;
—Psalm 148:7-8

The first time that stormy weather is mentioned in the Holy Scriptures it is to do with the judgment of Yah (God). It had never rained on the earth prior to the time that the flood happened in the days of Noah. That stormy weather called "the flood" annihilated the entire population of the earth in those early days, except for Noah and his immediate family, with a group of obedient and wise animals. Since then we can see that the Almighty consistently speaks His judgments to man through the weather.

As I was landing in Seoul, Korea, on the 24th of November 2005 having been sent by the Almighty from Jerusalem, Israel, I received the name of this book and the Scripture verse above. I had a clear and inner knowing that Yah (God) is eager to make us understand the times that we are living in. These are times of great upheavals, challenges and natural disasters. There are many voices trying to 'explain' what is happening in the world, in Israel and in the church. Why are we experiencing such stormy weather? Is it God? Is it the devil? Is it nature? I humbly suggest that we let the eternal word of the Creator and the obvious facts speak for themselves with a touch of updated prophetic input. My prayer is that everyone who reads this book will be enlightened enough to know what to do and how to respond during these both terrible and awesome times.

As I landed in Seoul, Korea, I was met by a very sunny, beautiful day and clear skies. Could it be that, in spite of this good sign, some more stormy weather is about to be released into the Far East and the world in general? How is this connected with Israel, the condition of the world, the condition of the church and the second coming of Messiah? Should we prepare for more stormy weather, or should we enjoy the sunny day and forget about it?

In Yeshua's amazing love,
Archbishop Dominiquae Bierman PhD
Jerusalem, Israel

CHAPTER ONE
Stormy Weather

"So pursue them with Your tempest, terrify them with Your storm. Fill their faces with confusion, that they may seek Your name, Yahveh."
—Psalm 83:15,16

The first time that stormy weather is mentioned in the Holy Scriptures it is to do with the judgment of Yah (God). It had never rained on the earth prior to the time that the flood happened in the days of Noah. That stormy weather called "the flood" annihilated the entire population of the earth in those early days, except for Noah and his immediate family with a group of obedient and wise animals. Since then we can see that the Almighty consistently speaks His judgments to man through the weather.

*On Friday the 13*th of August 2004 Rabbi Baruch and I were in a motel in Orlando, Florida. On that morning we had gone to a time-share presentation at one of the local holiday resorts that so abound in Orlando. Having been through these types of presentations before, we were pretty sure that we could get the benefits of it without letting it touch our pocketbooks. We arrived at the site early in the morning for there were clear threats of Hurricane Charlie coming our way, sometime in the afternoon or the evening. We were received, as usual, by a nice sales agent who later proceeded to tell us why Orlando, Florida, was the safest place to invest in property. He had a grin of self-satisfaction over his face as he drew on a piece of paper the "magic figure" of the one that kept Orlando stable - none other than Mickey Mouse!

We could hardly contain ourselves as he continued praising Disneyland as the key for the stability and financial soundness of Orlando, Florida...

Later on, back at the motel, on that same evening at 8.00 pm as Shabbat* was coming in, I began to close my notebook computer in the midst of writing my book "Grafted In" - calling the church to holiness and obedience to God's Commandments... As the sun set, exactly as Shabbat officially came in (the fourth Commandment!), so did Hurricane Charlie! It came in with a fury, uprooting fences, trees and houses on its path. It seemed that nothing could stand in the path of this terrible hurricane. On the following morning, the 14th of August, we rose up to behold the terrible devastation in Orlando and many other cities, as well as the many thousands of people who were left without housing, electricity and water. It was a sad day indeed as we bowed our hearts

---

* Shabbat - The fourth Commandment, the seventh day of rest and worship instilled by the Creator as He ended His creations. Shabbat has been kept by the Jewish people and desecrated by most of the church. During the time of Emperor Constantine, after the signing of the Council of Nicaea in year 325 AD that called for a divorce from the Jews and everything Jewish, the holy Shabbat was exchanged for Sunday because Constantine was a sun worshipper. In Isaiah 66:23 it says that all mankind will worship the Creator forever, every Shabbat.

in prayer for the suffering and at the same time uttering a shout of Halleluyah when we saw that our brand new van was standing intact in the parking lot with not even a leaf on it. Other cars did not enjoy the same fate as many seemed to be buried under trees and the like. Truly the Almighty had been faithful to His servants! So much for the stability of Mickey Mouse!

Exactly a year later...

On Sunday the 14th of August of 2005, the Ninth of Av, an annual day of mourning among Jews all over the world, commemorating the destruction of both the first and second temples and the offset of the terrible Spanish Inquisition, a special letter was hand-delivered via the USA Embassy in Tel Aviv to the then American Ambassador in Israel, Mr. Dan Kurtzer. This momentous day was merely the preparation day for the 15th of August, the day when the official Gaza and Gush Katif disengagement began. Teary eyes and torn hearts watched the TV as faithful Jewish settlers were being torn out from their houses by the hands of their own army and police. These people had spent twenty eight years making, what the local Arabs called "The Cursed Sands", to bloom. They invested their blood, sweat and tears to make a Garden of Eden of hothouses, under fire... And now they were being 'rewarded' by their own government, Mr. George W. Bush - the USA President, and the rest of the world community with being 'disengaged' from the land they married with their lives. Two weeks later Hurricane Katrina hit the

USA and destroyed the entire city of New Orleans. Some soothsayers said that there was no connection between these two events. However, on the 14th of August my letter with the word the Almighty had given me for President Bush stated that this was going to happen.

Mr. President of the USA
George W. Bush
9th of AV /14th of August 2005

Your Excellency,

The following word was given to me by the Lord God of Abraham, Isaac and Jacob, the God of Israel when He sent me to pray for you into the presidency of the USA as an Israeli. I am an Israeli Jewish-Christian bishop and regarded by many as a prophet.

This was before you were elected to be president for the first time. The votes were being recounted in Florida.

Through a series of events I found myself at the congressmen chapel at Speakers' Corner, with Ruth Mizel the widow of late Congressman Mizel.

Ruth and I knelt on the kneeling stools and I began to pray for you and said: "As an Israeli I call you into the Presidency of the United States."

Then the voice of the Lord came loud and clear to me; He said:

"If George W. Bush will do biblical politics concerning two issues:

1. The internal moral affairs of the United States
2. Israel

Then, he will be the most blessed president that the United States has ever had. But if not... (The Lord was silent at this point. The silence of God represents a sure judgment)

This is all He said.

Prior to the planned disengagement of Gaza on the 15th of August it is urgent that you would have this word, as your last-minute decision will affect you and the United States in a most serious manner. If you allow the uprooting of Gush Katif and Northern Samaria, judgment will surely follow.

Respectfully yours, Dr. Dominiquae Bierman

President of Kad-Esh MAP Ministries
Bishop of TAPAC, Jerusalem, Israel

Biblical Politics - Israel

"For behold, in those days and in that time, when I restore the fortunes of Judah and Jerusalem, I will gather all nations, and will bring them down into the valley of Jehoshaphat; And I will execute judgment on them there for My people, and for My heritage, Israel, whom they have scattered among the nations. They have divided My land."

—Joel 3:1-2

"For the day of Yahveh is near all the nations! As you have done, it will be done to you. Your deeds will return upon your own head."

—Obadiah 15

"For Yahveh has a day of vengeance, a year of recompense for the cause of Zion."

—Isaiah 34:8

"For thus says Yahveh of hosts: After glory has he sent me to the nations which plundered you; for he who touches you (Israel), touches the apple of His eye"

—Zechariah 2:8

"I will bring back the captivity of My people Israel, and they shall build the waste cities, and inhabit them, and they shall plant vineyards, and drink the wine of it; they shall also make gardens, and eat the fruit of them. I will plant them on their land, and they shall no more be plucked up out of their land which I have given them, says Yahveh your God."

—Amos 9:14-15

These extreme weather patterns seem to have accompanied the entire world immediately after the Gaza disengagement. Japan suffered from typhoons and bad winds and so did most of Europe. The city of Bern was flooded and so were other cities. Millions of dollars and yen, Swiss francs and the like were lost during these devastating days.

Target Florida

In September 2005 prior to the holiest day of the Scriptural calendar - Yom HaKippurim or the Day of The Atonements - I was summoned by the Almighty to "Target Florida". I was to begin to go to Florida sent by the spirit of God from Jerusalem bringing the message of repentance, as more "Stormy Weather" was on its way. The last time that Yahveh sent me to the USA was in the year 2,000 prior to the first election of President George W. Bush, when He warned me about the issue of "biblical politics" as I stated previously. When the Almighty sends me to any nation it is always about serious business and in order to call both the church (first) and the nation to repentance!

The doors opened up for me to preach in Naples, Florida, where people boasted that their place was totally 'safe' and that was also why their property values were so high, "because hurricanes never go through Naples". I felt a caution in my spirit and I still remember that as I preached in one of the local Hispanic congregations, I wept and warned them that I was afraid that if they did not take the message that

I brought seriously, judgment would surely follow. I called the church to repent and to be restored to the holiness, the fear of Yah (God) and the obedience to the Commandments that the early church in Jerusalem had... Later on, in October of the same year, during the celebrations of the Feast of Sukkoth (Tabernacles) in Israel, some of the saints in Naples, who heard my message and were then touring Israel with us, heard the frightening news that Hurricane Wilma was on its way to Miami and Naples, Florida. We prayed in Jerusalem for these precious ones that were with us and asked the Almighty to honor His word in Psalms 122:6, that as they came to bless Israel and to pray for Jerusalem, the Almighty would spare their houses. And so it was that the hurricane hit Naples, where hurricanes 'never happen', and the houses of all those that came to train and tour Israel with us were spared! One pastor from Naples had a tree fall parallel to his house and the house was left unharmed. Another couple from Miami reported to us that all the people around them were without electricity and water but not them! They were the only ones with electricity and water! Praise the living God whose word is eternal!

The Tsunami

It is said that when the last and most devastating tsunami hit the coasts of Thailand on Christmas weekend, the 26th of December of 2004, there was a little child that had been studying tsunamis at school. He noticed the receding waters as they uncovered the foundations of the coast. He immediately notified his parents that a tsunami was about to hit. The parents heeded the word of their child and they were rescued. Sadly, 300,000 others were not rescued and many of them are still buried in a watery grave and countless others will suffer for life from the after effects. Is there anyone who is reading this book that has the simple discernment of a little child to detect that there is more "Stormy Weather" to come? Or should we trust the Mickey Mouse fans and the Naples self-assured that everything will be AOK?

As I was in Naples calling the church there to repentance, I noticed that my first Sunday service fell on 9/11/2005, exactly four years after the destruction of the Twin Towers in New York on 9/11/2001. Later on, I received an SMS message on my cell phone from Israel. On that very same day - 9/11/2005 the Israeli flag was lowered over Gaza symbolizing the total retreat of Israel from those biblical lands that she made bloom against all odds. This was the outcome of an intense battle of terror against the Jewish state that began during September of 2000 (a year before the disaster of the Twin Towers). This terror war called Intifada had left Israel depleted of funds and extremely wounded. That in turn caused us to bow down to the demands of USA President George W. Bush and the quartet to give up Gaza in exchange for financial assistance. We were in the hole and the World Bank (based in Hong Kong in the Far East) had refused us any credit, so Uncle Sam came to the rescue with a letter of credit in exchange for Gaza, Samaria and East Jerusalem. A road map to the total destruction of Israel was underway. Is it any coincidence that the flag of Israel was being lowered over Gaza on the very same day that America was commemorating the tragedy of 9/11? Or was it a warning? Is there a connection between stormy weather, typhoons and hurricanes and between the escalating terrors in the nations? Is there any connection between the terror bombings of the underground in London around the same time that the USA was waking up to the nightmare of Katrina and the destruction of an entire city, and between the Gaza disengagement? Can it be that God's judgment has begun?

On Christmas Day of 2001 in Santiago, Chile, the Almighty visited me and told me that He will judge the nations according to these two principles:

1. His Righteous Laws and Commandments.

> For the wrath of God is revealed from heaven against all ungodliness and unrighteousness of men, who hinder the truth in unrighteousness, because that which is known of God is manifest in them; for God manifested it unto them. For the invisible things of Him since the creation of the world are clearly seen, being perceived through the things that are made, [even] His everlasting power and divinity; that they may be without excuse: because that, knowing God, they glorified Him not as God, neither gave thanks; but became vain in their reasonings, and their senseless heart was darkened. Professing themselves to be

wise, they became fools, and changed the glory of the incorruptible God for the likeness of an image of corruptible man, and of birds, and four-footed beasts, and creeping things. Wherefore God gave them up in the lusts of their hearts unto uncleanness, that their bodies should be dishonored among themselves: for that, they exchanged the truth of God for a lie, and worshipped and served the creature rather than the Creator, who is blessed forever. Amen. For this cause God gave them up unto vile passions: for their women changed the natural use into that which is against nature: And likewise, also the men, leaving the natural use of the woman, burned in their lust one toward another, men with men working unseemliness, and receiving in themselves that recompense of their error which was due. And even as they refused to have God in [their] knowledge, God gave them up unto a reprobate mind, to do those things which are not fitting; being filled with all unrighteousness, wickedness, covetousness, maliciousness; full of envy, murder, strife, deceit, malignity; whisperers, backbiters, hateful to God, insolent, haughty, boastful, inventors of evil things, disobedient to parents"
—Romans 1:18-30

The moral condition of the nations demands a serious response from a holy God who sent His son to die for us that we might repent from our own ways of wickedness. The world needs to wake up to the fact that it is running out of time, that these are the last minutes of grace from heaven before His wrath will be poured out - just like He did in ancient times when He destroyed Sodom and Gomorrah because of the idolatry, homosexuality, witchcraft and wickedness. The Most High has given us His best; His Holy son that whoever calls on His name - Yeshua the Messiah, can be saved from the wrath to come.

2. How the Nations Have Treated Israel, the Apple of His Eye.

For 2,000 years the nations and most particularly the Christians since the fourth century, have hated Israel and persecuted it in the Greek name - Jesus Christ. This kind of hatred culminated in the Spanish Inquisition and the Nazi Holocaust; both events having taken place in predominantly Christian nations - Catholic Spain and Protestant Germany. Nowadays, hatred of Jews is predominant all over the world and especially among the Muslims who would like the tiny nation of Israel destroyed and wiped off the map altogether. However, the last word remains with the Most High God who created Israel for His glory and who promised to destroy those that harm His people.

> "Ho Zion, escape you who dwell with the daughter of Babylon. For thus says Yahveh of hosts: After glory has he sent me to the nations which plundered

you; for he who touches you touches the apple of His eye."

—Zechariah 2:7,8

"I will bless those who bless you, and I will curse him who curses you. In you will all of the families of the earth be blessed."

—Genesis 12:3

After 2,000 years of hatred against the Jews, there are many nations that are about to incur God's judgment. These are the last minutes in the hourglass of the world to repent! He said that the *key for the blessing of all nations was to bless and do good to His Jewish people, the natural offspring of Abraham. This key that I call the Key of Abraham can open the blessing or the curse on the nations depending on their behavior with the Jews.*

I wrote a book called "Sheep Nations" as a fruit of this visitation and I encourage you to order it and to read it.

"As the days of Noah, so will be the coming of the son of man. For as in those days which were before the flood, they were eating and drinking, marrying and giving in marriage, until the day that Noah entered into the ark. And they didn't know until the flood came, and took them all away, so will be the coming of the son of man."

—Matthew 24:37-39

CHAPTER TWO
The Cause of Zion

God, don't keep silent. Don't keep silent and don't be still, God. For behold, your enemies are stirred up. Those who hate You have lifted up their heads. They conspire with cunning against Your people. They plot against Your cherished ones. "Come," they say, "and let us destroy them as a nation, that the name of Israel may be remembered no more." For they have conspired together with one mind. They form an alliance against You. The tents of Edom and the Ishmaelites; Moab, and the Hagrites; Gebal, Ammon, and Amalek; Philistia with the inhabitants of Tyre; Assyria also is joined with them. They have helped the children of Lot. Selah. Do to them as you did to Midian, As to Sisera, as to Jabin, at the river Kishon, who perished at Endor, who became as dung for the earth. Make their nobles like Oreb and Zeeb. Yes, all their princes like Zebah and Zalmunna, who said, "Let us take possession of God's pasturelands." My God, make them like tumbleweed; like chaff before the wind. As the fire that burns the forest, as the flame that sets the mountains on fire, so pursue them with Your tempest, terrify them with Your storm. Fill their faces with confusion, that they may seek Your name, Yahveh. Let them be put to shame and dismayed forever. Yes, let them be confounded and perish; that they may know

> *that you alone, whose name is Yahveh, are the Most High over all the earth.*
> —Psalm 83

We can see that the psalmist in Psalm 83 prays a prayer of judgment against those that hate Israel and he says, "So pursue them with Your tempest, terrify them with Your storm. Fill their faces with confusion, that they may seek Your name, Yahveh."

It seems to be that the psalmist is well aware of the use of winds, storms and tempests as an instrument of Yahveh's judgment. He also uses the word "terrify", in other words, brings forth terror. We can see an alarming connection here between terror and storms.

In the Book of Jeremiah we see that all of Israel's neighbors have one choice - to love Israel and the God of Israel (Yahveh not Allah!) or they will be utterly destroyed:

> "Thus says Yahveh against all My evil neighbors who touch the inheritance which I have caused My people Israel to inherit: behold, I will pluck them up from off their land, and will pluck up the house of Judah from among them. It shall happen, after that I have plucked them up, I will return and have compassion on them; and I will bring them again, every man to his heritage, and every man to his land. It shall happen, if they will diligently learn the ways of My

people, to swear by My name, as Yahveh lives; even as they taught My people to swear by Baal; then shall they be built up in the midst of My people. But if they will not hear, then will I pluck up that nation, plucking up and destroying it, says Yahveh."

—Jeremiah 12:14-17

Today, the Palestinians and all nations that are trying to take away the land of Israel that Yahveh Himself has caused Israel to inherit - against all odds and after the terrible Nazi Holocaust - are regarded as God's evil neighbors!

In Joel chapter 3, we read that the Almighty will enter into judgment with all the nations that divided Israel:

"For behold, in those days and in that time when I restore the fortunes of Judah and Jerusalem, I will gather all nations and will bring them down into the valley of Jehoshaphat. And I will execute judgment on them there for My people and for My heritage, Israel, whom they have scattered among the nations. They have divided My land,"

—Joel 3:1-2

In Obadiah we see that the Almighty repays every nation according to what has been done to Israel:

"For the violence done to your brother Jacob, shame will cover you, and you will be cut off forever. In the day that you stood on the other side, in the day that

> strangers carried away his substance, and foreigners entered into his gates, and cast lots for Jerusalem, even you were like one of them. But don't look down on your brother in the day of his disaster, and don't rejoice over the children of Judah in the day of their destruction. Don't speak proudly in the day of distress. Don't enter into the gate of My people in the day of their calamity. Don't look down on their affliction in the day of their calamity, neither seize their wealth on the day of their calamity. Don't stand in the crossroads to cut off those of His who escape. Don't deliver up those of his who remain on the day of distress. For the day of Yahveh is near all the nations! As you have done, it will be done to you. Your deeds will return upon your own head."
>
> —Obadiah 10-15

Is it a surprise that terror is running rampant all over the world? Is it therefore a surprise that the 9/11 2001 Twin Tower disaster in New York happened exactly a year after the outbreak of the Intifada in Jerusalem? Or that the underground in London was blown up by Islamic terrorists right after the beautiful settlements of Gush Katif in Gaza were evacuated and torn apart (as well as the hearts of the Jewish settlers). Mr. Tony Blair and President George W. Bush, were both members of the Quartet that implemented the Road Map and forced Israel to evacuate Gush Katif and Northern Samaria. In both instances Moslems and the Palestinians celebrated the destruction in the USA and London, while the Jews and the Israelis wept over their American and British friends who were wounded by terror. And yet these national leaders keep on pushing Israel to the limit and behaving unjustly. Yet it is the Almighty Himself whom they are pushing to the limit!

On the same day that Israel was relocating her dead in a heart-wrenching burial procession from the cemetery of Gush Katif in Gaza to the Mount of Olives in Jerusalem, the Iraqis were transporting coffins in a burial procession due to a terror attack in Baghdad. Around the same time it was reported that the waters of Hurricane Katrina had caused the tombs in New Orleans to be loosened and their dead were being 'relocated' into a watery grave.

During the Muslim month of Ramadan (30 days of fast to Allah) that fell in November this year of 2005, France suffered the beginning of an Intifada that may very well be the beginning of an Intifada all over Europe. The European Union has been giving millions of Euros in aid to the Palestinian cause and is one of the partners of the Quartet that imposed the Road Map on Israel. The outcome of the Road Map was the uprooting of the thriving settlements of Gush Katif in Gaza and others in Northern Samaria.

The following is taken from the Debka file reports:

> The violent riots spreading across France took several worrying directions Sunday night Nov. 6, and Monday (2005). The mostly Muslim gangs of

youths began surging out of the immigrant suburbs to invade town centers; they fired their first gunshots at policemen; the number of torched cars peaked to 1,400, and disturbing new slogans were hurled, depicting Paris as "Baghdad-on-the Seine" and their campaign as the start of Europe's Ramadan Intifada.

The following night, bands of marauding Muslim youths extended their areas of attack from outlying city districts to urban centers and started shooting at police officers.

The controlling hand, far from being a legitimate Muslim authority, is beginning to emerge as the very organization that has for several years been recruiting young fighters in French Muslim ghettos to fight Al Qaeda's wars against the West in Afghanistan, Bosnia, Iraq and other sectors.

On February 20, 2004, Debka-Net-Weekly and Debka file were the first to reveal the extent of Al Qaeda's penetration of West Europe. They turned up French intelligence statistics, which estimated that "Al Qaeda had recruited in France between 35,000 and 45,000 fighters and was organizing them in military-style units. They meet regularly for training in the use of weapons and explosives, combat tactics and indoctrination and are controlled from local and district command centers under the organization's national French command."

"In Germany, Al Qaeda's numbers are estimated at 25,000 to 30,000 men." Today, French counter-terror sources are willing to admit, albeit on the quiet and not for attribution, that those clandestine terrorist cells may well be at the bottom of the current riots. They note the history of the Palestinian uprising, which kicked off in 1987 with stones and petrol bombs, only to evolve into a suicide terrorist war by the late nineties. They fear this process may be beginning - not just in France but in the rest of Europe too, that the covert nucleus of trained and indoctrinated Islamic terrorists, Al Qaeda buried inside Europe, is being turned against the continent, starting in France.

For the day of Yahveh is near all the nations! As you have done, it will be done to you. Your deeds will return upon your own head."

—Obadiah, 15

Since Europe joined with the USA to pressure Israel to give away biblical land, it has suffered from very rough weather. A report from a staff member that lives part of the year in Bern, the Swiss capital city, reported that some areas of Bern were buried under the water of the devastating storms during the removal of the Jewish settlements in Gaza. Switzerland suffered over 800 million Swiss francs in damages. In general, from August 15th and on, the weather pattern in the world has been extremely rough with a lot more storms than usual. Japan, which gives aid to the Palestinian authorities, has suffered from several typhoons, as did Taiwan and China.

In Isaiah 34, He states through His prophet, that He has already destroyed all nations because of the cause of Zion:

> "Come near, you nations, to hear; and listen, you peoples: let the earth hear, and the fullness of it; the world, and all things that come forth from it. For Yahveh has indignation against all the nations, and wrath against all their host: He has utterly destroyed them, He has delivered them to the slaughter. Their slain also shall be cast out, and the stench of their dead bodies shall come up; and the mountains shall be melted with their blood. All the host of the sky shall be dissolved, and the heavens shall be rolled together as a scroll; and all their host shall fade away, as the leaf fades from off the vine, and as a fading [leaf] from the fig tree. For My sword has drunk its fill in the sky: behold, it shall come down on Edom, and on the people of My curse, to judgment. The sword of Yahveh is filled with blood, it is made fat with fatness, with the blood of lambs and goats, with the fat of the kidneys of rams; for Yahveh has a sacrifice in Bozrah, and a great slaughter in the land of Edom.

The wild-oxen shall come down with them, and the bulls with the bulls: and their land shall be drunken with blood, and their dust made fat with fatness. For Yahveh has a day of vengeance, a year of recompense for the cause of Zion."

—Isaiah 34:1-8

"Praise Yahveh from the earth, you great sea creatures, and all depths! Lightning and hail, snow and clouds. Stormy wind, fulfilling His word"

—Psalm 148:7,8

"For He breaks me with a tempest, multiplies my wounds without cause."

—Job 9:17

"Terrors overtake him like waters; A tempest steals him away in the night."

—Job 27:20

"Our God comes, and does not keep silence. A fire devours before Him. It is very Tempestuous around Him."

—Psalm 50:3

"I would hurry to a shelter from the stormy wind and tempest."

—Psalm 55:8

"So pursue them with Your tempest, terrify them with Your storm."

—Psalm 83:15

"Behold, the Lord has a mighty and strong one; as a tempest of hail, a destroying storm, as a tempest of mighty waters overflowing, will He cast down to the earth with the hand."

—Isaiah 28:2

"She shall be visited of Yahveh of hosts with thunder, and with earthquake, and great noise, with whirlwind and tempest, and the flame of a devouring fire."

—Isaiah 29:6

"Yahveh will cause His glorious voice to be heard, and will show the lighting down of His arm, with the indignation of [His] anger, and the flame of a devouring fire, with a blast, and tempest, and hailstones."

—Isaiah 30:30

CHAPTER THREE
Gaza and Katrina

For thou art a holy people unto the Lord thy God: the Lord thy God hath chosen thee to be a special people unto Himself, above all people that are upon the face of the earth.
—Deuteronomy 7:6

Dr. Terry Watkins from *Dial the Truth Ministries* writes: The destruction from hurricane Katrina unleashed a disaster like our nation has never encountered. Like a guided missile, Katrina executed a mission of utmost devastation. Despite our advancements in technology, computers, satellites, healthcare and tons of mind-boggling innovation the nation stood speechless and helpless.

It seemed everything that could go wrong – *went wrong. The breaking of the New Orleans levees; the thousands of trapped victims; the incessant looting; the perverse crime; the escalating gas prices; the complete collapse of the nation's infrastructure for disaster aid – each day after Katrina brought new nightmares – each day after Katrina whispered something terrible went wrong. The aftermath from Katrina plowed deeper and deadlier. Our nation and the entire world watched in disbelief as the nightmare from Katrina grew and held the world's most powerful nation hostage in her devastating grip. Many are asking, "Why? .... Why did God permit this tragedy?"*

If Katrina was indeed a severe warning from the Lord, the answer should not be difficult to find. I believe the answer clearly and precisely exists in the Scriptures...

Some Christians have aimed God's wrath of Katrina toward the gambling casinos of Mississippi or the cesspool of sin and sodomy raging in New Orleans. It's been noted that Katrina destroyed New Orleans just days before the depraved homosexual festival, appropriately called "Southern Decadence", was scheduled there. While a Holy God fiercely condemns and judges such sins, I don't believe that was Katrina's mission. Katrina did not merely destroy the casinos, or the hellholes and homosexual parade of New Orleans. No. Katrina was a warning for an entire nation. Katrina bruised and battered the soul of America.

Without question – for so many years, much like God's servant Job (Job 1:10), God placed a protective hedge around America. And like Job (Job 1:12), it appears God is removing His hedge.

On September 11, 2001, God removed His hedge around America. On September 11, 2001, God blinded the protective eyes of America. On that horrific day, America stood in "shock and awe" as over 2,700 people were brutally murdered by terrorists. Every precaution and prevention fell on deaf ears and blind eyes. Several reporters and commentators remarked it appeared as if "America was wearing blinders." Congress has appropriated hearing after hearing asking, "How did we miss the warning signals?" We didn't miss it. *We just couldn't see it. Something unusual and something terrible happened in America on September 11. The catastrophe was much worse than the tragedy of September 11 . . . God removed His protective* hedge.

What Really Occurred on September 11?

Several days prior to September 11, 2001, violent terrorists rocked Israel. I remember watching, on the news, the weeping Jewish mothers and fathers carrying the bodies of their children. Innocent children were literally blown apart simply because they were Jews. During this time the American administration forbade and threatened Israel with financial bribery if they retaliated. That Sunday on September 9, 2001, I remarked to the church; "if America keeps this hostile attitude toward Israel, America will suffer a major terrorist attack". Little did I realize, in two days America would suffer the greatest single terrorist attack in history...

Make no mistake about it – God has chosen the nation of Israel as His people. Whether you like it or not and whether you believe it or not – God's hand, both for His pleasure and His purpose, rests on the small nation of Israel.

For thou art a holy people unto the *Lord* thy God: the *Lord* thy God hath chosen thee to be a special people unto Himself, above all people that are upon the face of the earth.

—Deuteronomy 7:6

For the Lord hath chosen Jacob unto Himself, and Israel for His peculiar treasure.

—Psalm 135:4

But thou, Israel, art My servant, Jacob whom I have chosen, the seed of Abraham My friend.

—Isaiah 41:8

In 1917, after World War I, the famous Balfour Declaration set aside some land in Palestine as a homeland for the wandering Jews. But the Jews did not return. After the holocaust of Hitler resulting in the madness and murder of over 6 million Jews, they returned home. For hundreds of years, many Christians and Bible students discounted the promises from the Lord to rebuild and return Israel to their land. It just did not seem possible. But, "God is not a man, that He should lie; neither the son of man, that He should repent: hath He said, and shall He not do it? Or hath He spoken, and shall He not make it good?" (Numbers 23:19). In Isaiah 43, the Lord promised He would one day bring Israel back home. He would call them from the east, from the west, from the north and from the south.

After World War II, against all odds and against all obstacles – and there were many - exactly as the Lord prophesied, *from the east came Jews from Shanghai and Hong Kong; from the west came thousands of Jews from Egypt, Morocco, Tunis, Algeria, Europe, the United States and Latin America; from the north came over 20,000 Jews from Czechoslovakia, over 30,000 from Turkey, 36,000 from Bulgaria; and from the south came over 800,000 Jews from the land of the Arabs. The largest and most spectacular migration of a group of people occurred. As He promised, God was calling His people* home.

And in 1948, the greatest fulfillment of prophecy and the greatest miracle of the Scriptures since the resurrection of the Lord Jesus occurred – the "resurrection" of the nation of Israel. It's been said World War I prepared the land of Israel for the Jews, and World War II prepared the Jews for the land.

When the Lord God called out Abram and foretold the coming of Israel, God issued a severe warning concerning the treatment of the Jewish people, " . . . I will bless them that bless thee, and curse him that curse thee . . ." No other nation, no other people get such protection from the Lord.

God will judge His chosen people of Israel, as history testifies. But woe be to that nation or people that judges and deals hostilely with the Jewish people. The highways of history are littered with the remains of nations hostile to the Jews.

In Matthew 25, the Lord Jesus forewarns the "judgment of the nations" that will take place after the great tribulation. The nations are judged (verse 40) according to their treatment of "My brethren", of the Lord Jesus – the Jews.

Until recently, America has always been the best friend of Israel. It is no stretch to say if it wasn't for the protection and provision of America, Israel would not exist today. I have no doubt God wrought this great nation for the propagation of the glorious gospel of the Lord Jesus Christ and the protector and provider of His heritage, Israel.

The early 1990s marked a surprising and sickening departure from previous U.S. policy towards Israel. Beginning with President George H. Bush, more and more political pressure was placed upon Israel to surrender their land to the Palestinian terrorists.

The incredible book *Eye to Eye: Facing the Consequences of Dividing Israel by White House Correspondent William R. Koenig, proves many disasters befalling America come in direct and immediate response to George H. Bush, Bill Clinton and George W. Bush's devotion to robbing Israel of their God-given land. Koenig documents the following incredible facts occur because of the U.S.'s pressure to evacuate Israel from their* land:

1. Nine of the ten costliest insurance events in U.S. history
2. Six of the seven costliest hurricanes in U.S. history
3. Three of the four largest tornado outbreaks in U.S. history
4. Nine of the top ten natural disasters in U.S. history ranked by FEMA relief costs
5. The two largest terrorism events in U.S. history

Amazon.com says, "All of these major catastrophes transpired on the very same day or within 24 hours of

U.S. presidents Bush, Clinton and Bush applying pressure on Israel to trade her land for promises of "peace and security," sponsoring major "land for peace" meetings, making major public statements pertaining to Israel's covenant land and/or calling for a Palestinian state . . . In this book, Bill Koenig provides undeniable facts and conclusive evidence showing that indeed the leaders of the United States and the world are on a collision course with God over Israel's covenant land."

Koenig's book was published in 2004. In a bit of prophetic irony, on the cover of his book, *Eye to Eye: Facing the Consequences of Dividing Israel*, he shows a grim-faced President Bush turning his eyes as a massive hurricane appears.

The following events paint a picture of hypocrisy and hostility towards Israel and defiance against the word of God, beginning with President George H. Bush in 1991. Immediately following these political assaults against Israel occurred some of the most catastrophic disasters in the history of the United States. To ascribe the disasters at these precise hours as coincident or random chance, breaks the sound barrier of statistical probability. The possibility of these many major catastrophes happening by haphazard chance at these precise times is simply impossible.

You want proof the Bible is the word of God, here's your proof. You want proof Israel is God's heritage here's your proof.

1991 30 October - The Oslo Accord

President George H. Bush promoted and proudly signed the infamous Oslo Accord at the Madrid Peace Conference on October 30, 1991. The Oslo Accord was labeled a "Land for Peace" accord that demanded Israel award their land to the Palestinian murderers and terrorists in exchange for peace. The perverse Oslo proposition was simple: give us your land and we'll stop killing you.

1991 31 October - The Next Day – The Perfect Storm Hits

A very rare and huge storm starting in the north Atlantic, moving east to west (wrong direction for storms to move - although in the Bible, the Holy Spirit and history move east to west). This storm was so unusual and contrary to "mother nature" it was immortalized by the book *The Perfect Storm* by Sebastian Junger and later a popular movie. Amazon says of the book *The Perfect Storm*, "Meteorologists called the storm that hit North America's eastern seaboard in October 1991 a "perfect storm" because of the rare combination of factors that created it. For everyone else, it was perfect hell. In *The Perfect Storm*, author Sebastian Junger conjures for the reader the meteorological conditions that created the "storm of the century" and the impact the storm had on many of the people caught in it.

Interesting, one of the first places *The Perfect Storm* hit was Kennebunkport, Maine. Waves over 30 feet demolished the home of, guess who, President George H. Bush, the instigator of the Oslo Accord.

1992 23 August

A year later, President Bush literally picked up the pieces from Oslo, attempting to rob Israel again. Meeting in Washington D.C., Bush and crew again attempted to "sell" the fictitious Madrid "Land for Peace" agreement.

1992 23 August – Same Day - Hurricane Andrew Visits Florida

Hurricane Andrew smashes and crashes Florida. Andrew causes over $30 billion in damage while destroying over 180,000 homes. At that time, Andrew was the worst natural disaster ever to hit America.

1994 16 January

President Bill Clinton meets with terrorist and Israel hater, President of Syria, Hafez el-Assad in Geneva. They talk about a peace agreement with Israel that includes Israel giving up the Golan Heights.

1994 17 January – Less Than 24 hours - 6.9 Earthquake Rocks California

In less than 24 hours, a powerful 6.9 earthquake rocks Southern California. This mysterious quake, centered in Northridge, is the second most destructive natural disaster to hit the United States, behind Hurricane Andrew.

1998 21 January

Israeli Prime Minister Benjamin Netanyahu meets with President Clinton at the White House and is coldly received. Clinton and Secretary of State Madeleine Albright refuse to have lunch with him.

1998 21 January – The Same Day - Monica Lewinsky Scandal Erupts

After Clinton's rejection of Israeli Prime Minister Benjamin Netanyahu, later the very same day, the

Monica Lewinsky scandal breaks out, destroying the Clinton presidency and resulting in his impeachment.

Before proceeding let us clarify who truthfully owns the Gaza Strip and West Bank. God does. He calls it "My land." Joel 3, deals *exactly with this issue. The Lord clearly states in no uncertain terms, He will "plead" with the nations such as the United States that "scatters" Israel and "parts His land."* That is as much the Word of God as John 3:16. And the United States is not exempt – "all nations" means "all nations".

> For behold, in those days and in that time, when I shall bring again the captivity of Judah and Jerusalem, I will also gather all nations, and will bring them down into the valley of Jehoshaphat, and will plead with them there for My people and for My heritage Israel, whom they have scattered among the nations, and parted My land.
>
> —Joel 3:1-2

In case you think "the land of Israel" became unimportant since the New Testament – think again. Galatians 4 deals with "the land" and the Lord says clearly and plainly, the land belongs to Isaac – not the Arabs.

For it is written, that Abraham had two sons, the one by a bondmaid, the other by a freewoman. But he who was of the bondwoman was born after the flesh, but he of the freewoman was by promise. Which things are an allegory: for these are the two covenants; the one from the mount Sinai, which gendereth to bondage, which is Agar. For this Agar is mount Sinai in Arabia, and answereth to Jerusalem, which now is, and is in bondage with her children. But Jerusalem which is above is free, which is the mother of us all. For it is written, rejoice, thou barren that bearest not; break forth and cry, thou that travailest not: for the desolate hath many more children than she who hath a husband. Now we, brethren, as Isaac was, are the children of promise. But as then he that was born after the flesh persecuted him that was born after the spirit, even so it is now. Nevertheless what saith the Scripture? Cast out the bondwoman and her son (Arabs): for the son of the bondwoman shall not be heir with the son (Jews) of the freewoman.

—Galatians 4:22-30

With that settled, let us continue...

1998 28 September

Secretary of State Madeleine Albright finishes the final details of an agreement that requires Israel to surrender 13 percent of Yesha (Judah and Samaria).

President Bill Clinton meets with Yasser Arafat and Netanyahu at the White House to finalize another Israel "land for peace" hoodwink. Later, Arafat addresses the United Nations and declares an independent Palestinian state by May 1999.

1998 28 September – Same Day - Hurricane George Hits Gulf Coast

Hurricane George blasts the Gulf Coast with 110 mph winds and gusts up to 175 mph. The hurricane hit the coast and stalled until the agreement was finalized and Arafat addressed the UN. Then it hit and caused $1 billion in damage. At the exact time that Arafat departs the U.S., the storm begins to dissipate.

1998 15 October

Arafat and Netanyahu meet at the Wye River Plantation in Maryland. The talks are scheduled to last five days with the focus on Israel giving up 13 percent of Yesha. The talks are extended and conclude on October 23.

1998 17 October – Two Days Later - Tornadoes Hit Texas

On October 17, heavy storms and tornadoes hit southern Texas. The San Antonio area is deluged with rain. The rain and flooding in Texas continue until October 22 and then subside. The floods ravage 25 percent of Texas and leave over one billion dollars in damage. On October 21, Clinton declares this section of Texas a major disaster area.

1998 30 November

Arafat arrives in Washington again to meet with President Clinton to raise money for a Palestinian state with Jerusalem as the capital. A total of 42 other nations were represented in Washington. All the nations agreed to give Arafat $3 billion in aid. Clinton promised $400 million, and the European nations $1.7 billion.

1998 30 November – Same Day - Financial Disaster

The Dow Jones average drops 216 points, and on December 1, the European Market had its third worst day in history. Hundreds of billions of market capitalization were wiped out in the U.S. and Europe.

1998 12 December

President Clinton arrives in the Palestinian-controlled section of Israel to discuss another "land for peace" fiasco.

1998 12 December – Same Day - Clinton impeached

The U.S. House of Representatives votes four articles of impeachment against President Clinton.

1999 3 May

Yasser Arafat schedules a press conference to announce a Palestinian state with Jerusalem as the capital.

1999 3 May - Same Day - Powerful Storms in Oklahoma and Kansas

The most powerful tornado storm system ever to hit the United States whips through Oklahoma and Kansas. The winds are clocked at 316 mph, the fastest wind speed ever recorded. Arafat postpones his announcement to December 1999 at the request of buddy President Clinton. In his letter to Arafat, Clinton praises and encourages Arafat for his "aspirations for his own land."

2001 8 June

President George W. Bush sends Secretary Tenet to Jerusalem to promote his "Roadmap to Peace," the continuation of the failed Oslo Accord.

2001 8 June – Same Day - Tropical Storm Allison Hits Texas

Tropical storm Allison hits Texas the home state of President George W. Bush. Allison causes over $7 billion in damage and closes George Bush Airport for two days. Allison continues for five long days. When Tenet leaves Jerusalem, Allison settles down.

The following series of events during August – September of 2001 preceded history's deadliest terrorist attack.

2001 23 August

President George W. Bush rips Yasser Arafat on *CNN. Bush suggests that Arafat "put 100% effort into stopping terrorism" if he wants Israel to negotiate. Saudi leader Abdullah is incensed. He tells Ambassador Bandar to immediately leave the U.S. because Bush supports* Israel.

2001 27 August

On his way out, Bandar meets with Condi Rice while Bush is on vacation. Bandar tells Rice how unacceptable Bush's comments were, threatens to withhold oil, and says that he's leaving in disgust. Condi reports to President Bush, who immediately issues a written letter to Bandar stating "Palestinian people have the right to live in their own state, in their own homeland."

2001 7 September

Eleven days later, a jubilant Bandar returns to America and meets with Bush, Cheney, Rice, and Powell to hammer out the details and announce to the world the creation of the Palestinian state. The negotiations and details continue until September 9, 2001.

2001 10 September

Bandar and crew finish President Bush's plans to create a Palestinian nation in Israel in 2005. Bandar calls his offices to inform them the agreement is finally finished.

2001 11 September – Next Day - Terrorists Explode into the World Trade Center

8:45 a.m. (EDT) American Airlines Flight 11 out of Boston, Massachusetts, crashes and explodes into the north tower of the World Trade Center.

9:03 a.m. (EDT) United Airlines Flight 175 from Boston crashes and explodes into the south tower of the World Trade Center. Both Towers come crashing down. Flashed across televisions around the globe, the world witnessed the greatest terrorist act in history. Over 2700 people die in a few short minutes.

9:43 a.m. (EDT) American Airlines Flight 77 crashes into the Pentagon.

Certainly, the Lord Knew the Coming Devastation & Death From Katrina

The Scriptures reveal many "natural" disasters as instruments of wrath from the hand of God. The fire and brimstone raining down and destroying Sodom and Gomorrah promptly comes to mind. Let us not forget that the wrath of God once exterminated every breath on the whole earth, yet He saved Noah and his family. The Old Testament testifies over and over of the judgment of God. King David bows to the temptation of Satan to number Israel and an angry God kills 70,000 men (1 Chron. 21:14). We read of God's hand in the divine destruction of Jericho (Joshua 6:20), the termination of the kingdoms of Babylon, Assyria, Egypt, and the Amalekites (1 Samuel 15:8) among many others.

The Scriptures establish that God creates, controls and even commands the weather. Amos 4:13 says "For lo, He that formeth the mountains and createth the wind . . ." Many times, God specifically employs the wind to preach His message. Just ask a backslidden prophet named Jonah. Jonah 1:4 says "But the Lord sent out a great wind into the sea, and there was a mighty tempest in the sea, so that the ship was like to be broken." Ask the fearful apostles after watching the Lord Jesus calmly rebuke " . . a great storm of wind. . . and said unto the sea, peace, be still. And the wind ceased, and there was a great calm." The Bible records the amazed apostles, "And they feared exceedingly, and said one to another "What manner of man is this, that even the wind and the sea obey Him?" (Mark 4:41)

The Scriptures many times reveal the Lord God utilizes the wind as His instrument of action. In fact, of all the environmental resources at His omnipotent disposal, the wind emerges as His first choice. The following Scriptures, among scores of others, provide our proof:

Therefore thus saith the Lord *God;* I will even rend it with a stormy wind in My fury; and there shall be an overflowing shower in Mine anger, and great hailstones in My fury to consume it. And the Lord shall utterly destroy the tongue of the Egyptian sea; and with His mighty wind shall He shake His hand over the river, and shall smite it in the seven streams, and make men go over dryshod.

—Isaiah 11:15

Thus saith the Lord, Behold, I will raise up against Babylon, and against them that dwell in the midst of them that rise up against Me, a destroying wind..

—Jeremiah 51:1

Katrina was no accident. Katrina was no haphazard natural disaster. Katrina was no climatic coincident of mother nature. Katrina was a warning from the Lord.

Remember, Katrina had to come with the foreknowledge and provision of God. To reason otherwise rejects the Scriptures, and denies the sovereign presence of a Holy, Almighty God.

With that as our solid foundation we can now ask, "Why did God allow Katrina to shatter America?" And more important, "What message from the Lord was wrapped in Katrina?"

Can we dare attempt to answer such a question? Not only can we – we *Must*!

If the Lord is sending America a message – it is critical... it is essential for us to "find the message."

Middle East scholar, Robert Horenstein spoke on Israel's disengagement from Gaza on September 21 at the meeting of the Golda Meir/Mitzvah group of Hadassah.

Horenstein stated, "If Israel does carry out this withdrawal, you will see the violence stepped up because Hamas, Islamic Jihad, the Al-Aksa Martyrs Brigade will want to show their people that Israel is leaving as a result of their terrorist actions. They have already claimed Sharon's proposal is a result of their armed struggle. I believe that Israel is under a lot of pressure from the Bush administration. . ."

A Haifa University demographer, Arnon Soffer, had projected that by 2015 all of Israel, the Gaza Strip and the West Bank will be 60 percent Arab, and this would make it impossible for Israel to retain both its democratic and Jewish character."

(Jewish Review, "Disengagement could spawn civil, external violence")

At the Mideast summit in Jordan on June 4, Israeli Prime Minister Ariel Sharon and Palestinian Prime Minister Mahmoud Abbas took the first tentative verbal steps toward a peaceful resolution of their longstanding and bloody conflict. Under pressure from President Bush, Mr. Sharon pledged to begin dismantling some "unauthorized outposts" of Israeli settlements in the West Bank, and Mr. Abbas declared for the first time "the armed intifada must end."

Over the last week, emotional scenes of Jewish settlers being forcibly removed have dominated the television headlines. Israeli Prime Minister Ariel Sharon has talked of how these have been the "saddest days" of his life, and the words "pogrom" and "dispossessed" have slowly slipped into the language of many newspaper reports . . .

The Palestinian authority and the United States want the pullout to be the beginning of the "road map" peace process, meant to bring about an independent Palestinian state alongside Israel. ("Israeli Force Storms Synagogue")

The Gaza withdrawal was backed by the U.S. government. Some Middle East analysts and senior Israeli politicians entirely attributed the evacuation plan to pressure coming from the American establishment . . . "I welcome the disengagement plan," stated Bush immediately following the announcement of the Gaza evacuation. "These steps will mark real progress toward realizing the vision I set forth in June 2002 of two states living side by side in peace and security."

50 – Stormy Weather

2005 August - Under U.S. pressure, the Jews are forcibly removed from their land.

During the month of August 2005, with unparalleled pressure from the United States – the dreaded D-day came. Over 8,500 begging Jewish settlers were forcibly removed from the Gaza Strip. I watched in unbelief as the Jewish people were crying and pleading to remain in their houses and land. The Israeli soldiers came and literally dragged them from their houses. At the orders of the United States and against the protests of the Israeli government, bulldozers came and demolished their homes. The land was then given to terrorists who celebrated and shouted, "Death to Israel!"

US Secretary of State Condoleezza Rice told BBC News, "Jewish homes in the Gaza Strip will be destroyed when Israel pulls out its troops and settlers . . . The view is that there are better land uses for the Palestinians to better address their housing needs," adding that the parties would "work towards a plan for destruction and clean-up."

After the Gaza Strip debacle, US Secretary of State Condoleezza Rice immediately began urging Israel to vacate the West Bank, "Everyone has compassion for what the Israelis are going through right now, but it can't stop with the Gaza Strip."

The hypocrisy and hostility towards the nation of Israel by the Bush administration are unparalleled in U.S. history. Violently removing the Jewish settlers from the Gaza Strip, then giving the land to the terrorists and murderers of Israeli children equates to Bush giving Florida to Bin Laden and Al-Qaeda.

Why didn't President Bush give Saddam Hussein the land of Texas instead of bombing Iraq? That would be more logical than demanding Israel to forfeit a strategic defense area of the Gaza Strip and West Bank to vicious killers that hate and kill the Jews.

2005 23 August

Israel completed the evacuation of the Gaza Strip and gave it to the Palestinians. The Gaza Strip evacuation came directly from President Bush's "Roadmap to Peace."

As my wife and I watched the pleading Jews dragged from their homes and land, I said, "God is not pleased with this. Somebody's gonna pay big-time for this. God might start destroying some homes and running some people out of their land."

And somebody did . . . and boy did they.

2005 23 August – the Same Day - Tropical Storm Katrina appears

On August 23, a small insignificant tropical storm slowly appeared in the Atlantic below the Bahamas named Katrina. From her beginning meteorologists stated the U.S. had nothing to fear. Katrina packed little punch, plus the computer forecasts kept Katrina calmly corralled in the Atlantic. Defying the computer models, Katrina turned southeast, scraped the south tip of Florida and then with the vengeance of a runaway freight train Katrina took an unexpected turn into the warm Gulf Coast. Meteorologists tracking Katrina's unusual path labeled Katrina one of history's most bizarre hurricanes.

2005 29 August - Hurricane Katrina hits New Orleans

Katrina raced directly toward New Orleans, harnessing deadly strength every moment. Literally recording wind strength "off the scale" on Monday, August 29, the nation watched in horror as deadly Katrina slammed and slaughtered the fragile Gulf Coast. Destructive Katrina left beautiful homes as piles of worthless rubbish. Deadly Katrina tossed bodies like litter along the highway. When Katrina ended her deadly mission America suffered the worst disaster in her storied history. As I saw the thousands of homes destroyed, my mind kept going back to those U.S.-ordered bulldozers destroying the Jewish homes in the Gaza Strip. As I saw the thousands and thousands of United States citizens being evacuated from their land, my mind could not keep from remembering the Jewish people crying and literally begging to stay in their land. America found no mercy for the Jewish people . . .

With no mercy . . . Katrina completely "bulldozed" tens of thousands of homes. Katrina completely "evacuated" the celebrated city of New Orleans. Hundreds of thousands are homeless, helpless and hopeless. The greatest displacement of

U.S. citizens in history occurred. Over 10,000 people are estimated dead. Over 400,000 jobs were wiped out. President Bush has requested $50 billion from Congress for the first round of Katrina's expensive bill. Estimates put Katrina's final bill – over $150 billion.

Most reporters described the aftermath of New Orleans worse than anything they've ever seen.

If America continues to blatantly defy the word of God with their hostility and hypocrisy toward God's heritage, Israel, buckle up . . . you ain't seen nothing yet.

(End of quote from Dr. Terry Watkins, includes excerpts from White House Correspondent Bill Koenig's book *Eye to Eye* and a quote by Middle East Scholar Mr. Robert Horenstein) ("Katrina: Mother Nature or the Wrath of God?")

"Behold, the tempest of Yahveh, [even His] wrath, is gone forth, a sweeping tempest: it shall burst on the head of the wicked."

—Jeremiah 30:23

I hope that by now you are convinced that the Creator is the author of tempests and He uses them as a weapon of judgment and especially judgment on the nations for touching His people Israel and dividing His land.*

Thus says Yahveh of hosts, Behold, evil shall go forth from nation to nation, and a great tempest shall be raised up from the uttermost parts of the earth."

—Jeremiah 25:32

---

*   For an important prophetic word concerning this, please go to our website www.kad-esh.org and click on prophecies, then see a prophecy from Wendy Alec - September 23, 2005, Hurricane Katrina:- America I am charging you repent. A hard message – A message of flint.

CHAPTER FOUR
Weapons of Mass Destruction

"Behold, I have created the smith who blows the fire of coals, and brings forth a weapon for his work; and I have created the waster to destroy. No weapon that is formed against you shall prosper; and every tongue that shall rise against you in judgment you shall condemn. This is the heritage of the servants of Yahveh, and their righteousness which is of Me, says Yahveh."
—Isaiah 54:16-17

The HAARP Project

Yahveh has made Himself known. He has executed judgment. The wicked is snared by the work of his own hands.
—Psalm 9:16

H.A.A.R.P. (High frequency Active Auroral Research Project), looks to the naked eye as an innocent research project; composed of 36 antennas erected in central Alaska about 300 Km East of Anchorage (62 degrees 23.5'N, 145 degrees 8.8'W).*

It's not only greenhouse gas emissions: Washington's new world order weapons have the ability to trigger climate change.

By Michel Chossudovsky: Professor of Economics, University of Ottawa and TFF associate, author of *The Globalization of Poverty, second edition, Common Courage Press*

The important debate on global warming under UN auspices provides but a partial picture of climate change; in addition to the devastating impacts of greenhouse gas emissions on the ozone layer, the world's climate can now be modified as part of a new system of sophisticated "non-lethal weapons." Both the Americans and the Russians have developed capabilities to manipulate the world's climate. In the US, the technology is being perfected under the High-frequency Active Aural Research Program (HAARP), as part of the ("Star Wars") Strategic Defense Initiative (SDI). Recent scientific evidence suggests that HAARP is fully operational and has the ability of potential to trigger floods, droughts, hurricanes and earthquakes.

* http://www.transnational.org/forum/meet/2000/Chossu_Green HouseHAARP.html

HAARP is a mass destructive weapon

From a military standpoint, HAARP is a weapon of mass destruction. Potentially, it constitutes an instrument of conquest capable of selectively destabilizing agricultural and ecological systems of entire regions. While there is no evidence that this deadly technology has been used, surely the United Nations should be addressing the issue of "environmental warfare" alongside the debate on the climatic impacts of greenhouse gases. Despite a vast body of scientific knowledge, the issue of deliberate climatic manipulations for military use, has never been explicitly part of the UN agenda on climate change. Neither the official delegations nor the environmental action groups participating in the Hague Conference on Climate Change (CO6) (November 2000) have raised the broad issue of "weather warfare" or "environmental modification techniques (ENMOD)" as relevant to an understanding of climate change.

"Weather Warfare"

World-renowned scientist Dr. Rosalie Bertell confirms, "US military scientists are working on weather systems as a potential weapon. The methods include the enhancing of storms and the diverting of vapor rivers in the Earth's atmosphere to produce targeted droughts or floods."*

Already in the 1970s, former National Security advisor Zbigniew Brzezinski had foreseen in his book "Between Two Ages" that: "Technology will make available to the leaders of major nations, techniques for conducting secret warfare, of which only a bare minimum of the security forces need be appraised... Techniques of weather modification could be employed to produce prolonged periods of drought or storm."

Marc Filterman, a former French military officer, outlines several types of "unconventional weapons" using radio frequencies. He refers to "weather war" indicating that the U.S. and the Soviet Union had already "mastered the know-how needed to unleash sudden climate changes (hurricanes, drought) in the early 1980s." ** These technologies make it "possible to trigger atmospheric disturbances by using Extremely Low Frequency (ELF) radar [waves]."***

A simulation study of future defense "scenarios" commissioned for the US Air Force calls for: "US aerospace forces to 'own the weather' by capitalizing

---

*   The Times, London, 23 November 2000.
** Intelligence Newsletter, December 16, 1999.
*** Ibid.

on emerging technologies and focusing development of those technologies to war-fighting applications." From enhancing friendly operations or disrupting those of the enemy via small-scale tailoring of natural weather patterns to complete dominance of global communications and counterspace control, weather-modification offers the war fighter a wide range of possible options to defeat or coerce an adversary. In the United States, weather modification will likely become a part of national security policy with both domestic and international applications. Our government will pursue such a policy, depending on its interests, at various levels.*

The High-Frequency Active Aural Research Program (HAARP) based in Gokoma, Alaska - jointly managed by the US Air Force and the US Navy - is part of a new generation of sophisticated weaponry under the US Strategic Defense Initiative (SDI). Operated by the Air Force Research Laboratory's Space Vehicles Directorate, HAARP constitutes a system of powerful antennas capable of creating "controlled local modifications of the ionosphere".

Scientist Dr. Nicholas Begich, actively involved in the public campaign against HAARP, describes HAARP as "A super powerful radio wave-beaming

---

* Air University of the US Air Force, AF 2025 Final Report, http://www.au.af.mil/au/2025/ (emphasis added).

technology lifts areas of the ionosphere [upper layer of the atmosphere] by focusing a beam and heating those areas. Electromagnetic waves then bounce back onto earth and penetrate everything - living and dead." *

Dr. Rosalie Bertell depicts HAARP as "a gigantic heater that can cause major disruption in the ionosphere, creating not just holes, but long incisions in the protective layer that keeps deadly radiation from bombarding the planet." **

Misleading Public Opinion

HAARP has been presented to public opinion as a program of scientific and academic research. US military documents seem to suggest, however, that HAARP's main objective is to "exploit the ionosphere for Department of Defense purposes."

***Without explicitly referring to the HAARP program, a US Air Force study points to the use of "induced ionospheric modifications" as a means of

---

* Nicholas Begich and Jeane Manning, The Military's Pandora's Box, Earthpulse Press, http://www.xyz.net/~nohaarp/earthlight.html. See also the HAARP home page at http://www.haarp.alaska.edu/).

** See Briarpatch, January, 2000. (emphasis added).

*** Quoted in Begich and Manning, op cit.

altering weather patterns as well as disrupting enemy communications and radar.*

According to Dr. Rosalie Bertell, HAARP is part of an integrated weapons' system, which has potentially devastating environmental consequences: "It is related to fifty years of intensive and increasingly destructive programs to understand and control the upper atmosphere. It would be rash not to associate HAARP with the space laboratory construction that is separately being planned by the United States. HAARP is an integral part of a long history of space research and development of a deliberate military nature.

The military implications of combining these projects are alarming. The ability of the HAARP/Space lab/rocket combination to deliver very large amounts of energy, comparable to a nuclear bomb, anywhere on earth via laser and particle beams, is frightening. The project is likely to be "sold" to the public as a space shield against incoming weapons, or, for the more gullible, a device for repairing the ozone layer."**

In addition to weather manipulation, HAARP has a number of related uses: "HAARP could contribute

---

* Air University, op cit.

** Rosalie Bertell, Background of the HAARP Program, 5 November, 1996, http://www.globalpolicy.org/socecon/envronmt/weapons.htm

to climate change by intensively bombarding the atmosphere with high-frequency rays. Returning low-frequency waves at high intensity could also affect people's brains, and effects on tectonic movements cannot be ruled out.*

More generally, HAARP has the ability of modifying the World's electromagnetic field. It is part of an arsenal of "electronic weapons" which US military researchers consider a "gentler and kinder warfare." **

Weapons of the New World Order

HAARP is part of the weapons arsenal of the New World Order under the Strategic Defense Initiative (SDI).

From military command points in the US, entire national economies could potentially be destabilized through climatic manipulations. More importantly, the latter can be implemented without the knowledge of the enemy, at minimal cost and without engaging military personnel and equipment as in a

---

*   Begich and Manning, op cit.

**   Don Herskovitz, Killing Them Softly, Journal of Electronic Defense, August 1993. (emphasis added). According to Herskovitz, "electronic warfare" is defined by the US Department of Defense as "military action involving the use of electromagnetic energy." The Journal of Electronic Defense at http://www.jedefense.com/ has published a range of articles on the application of electronic and electromagnetic military technologies.

conventional war. The use of HAARP - if it were to be applied - could have potentially devastating impacts on the world's climate.

Responding to US economic and strategic interests, it could be used to selectively modify climate in different parts of the world resulting in the destabilization of agricultural and ecological systems. It is also worth noting that the US Department of Defense has allocated substantial resources to the development of intelligence and monitoring systems on weather changes. NASA and the Department of Defense's National Imagery and Mapping Agency (NIMA) are working on "imagery for studies of flooding, erosion, land-slide hazards, earthquakes, ecological zones, weather forecasts, and climate change" with data relayed from satellites.*

We need to establish as a foundation that all weapons of mass destruction have been created by Yahveh. Neither man nor devil can create anything; they are not the Creator! Far too many people ascribe to the devil powers that he does not possess and exalt him above the Almighty. Yahveh-God is the sole and only Creator and there is none other! He created the Tree of Life but He also created the Tree of Knowledge of Good and Evil that caused the Fall of Adam. He created the holy angels but He also created Lucifer who became Satan.

* Military Source, 6 December, 1999.

He created man, but He also created the capacity for man to pervert himself if he so wished. He created the sparrow but He also created the snakes with a poison capable to kill men. He created Heaven but He also created Hell. He is the awesome All Powerful, Most Highly Exalted Creator to be feared and there is none other.

> "I form the light, and create darkness; I make peace, and create evil. I am Yahveh, who does all these things."
>
> —Isaiah 45:7

He created the evil for the day of judgment; He is the one who sent the angel of death upon the Egyptians and spared His own people Israel because of the blood of the lamb on the doorposts.

> "For I will go through the land of Egypt in that night, and will strike all the firstborn in the land of Egypt, both man and animal. Against all the gods of Egypt I will execute judgments: I am Yahveh. The blood shall be to you for a token on the houses where you are: and when I see the blood, I will pass over you, and there shall no plague be on you to destroy you when I strike the land of Egypt."
>
> —Exodus 12:12-13

The God of Israel is so jealous over His judgments and deliverance feats that He wants them remembered forever!

"This day shall be to you for a memorial, and you shall keep it a feast to Yahveh: throughout your generations you shall keep it a feast by an ordinance forever."

—Exodus 12:14

It was Yahveh who sent a pestilence over Israel at the time of King David because of the iniquity of His own people. He even moved King David to sin before Him by numbering the people, so that He could send His punishment:

"Again the anger of Yah was kindled against Israel, and He moved David against them saying, Go, number Israel and Judah". "So Yahveh sent a pestilence on Israel from the morning even to the time appointed, and there died of the people from Dan even to Beersheba seventy thousand men. When the angel stretched out his hand toward Jerusalem to destroy it, Yahveh repented him of the evil, and said to the angel who destroyed the people, It is enough; now stay your hand. The angel of Yahveh was by the threshing floor of Araunah the Jebusite."

—2 Samuel 24:1,15,16

"Behold, I have created the smith who blows the fire of coals, and brings forth a weapon for his work, and I have created the waster to destroy."

—Isaiah 54:16

We can see that the only one that has power to withhold or permit evil is none other than the Almighty Himself, however, He spreads a special protection over those who fear Him,

> "The fear of Yahveh [tendeth] to life; And He [that hath it] shall abide satisfied; He shall not be visited with evil."
> —Proverbs 19:23 Standard Version

> "The fear of Yahveh leads to life, then contentment; He rests and will not be touched by trouble".
> —Proverbs 19:23 World English Version

> Therefore the wicked shall not stand in the judgment, nor sinners in the congregation of the righteous.
> —Psalm 1:5

Since we now know that the Almighty is the only Creator of both good and evil, how can we relate to the wicked schemes of man such as the HAARP project? It is obvious that man tries to set himself up as God, trying to manipulate the weather patterns. This kind of occurrence has happened in the past; let us see what the reaction of the Almighty was:

> "The whole earth was of one language and of one speech. It happened, as they journeyed east, that they found a plain in the land of Shinar; and they lived there. They said one to another, "Come, let's

make brick, and burn them thoroughly." They had brick for stone, and they used tar for mortar. They said, "Come, let's build us a city, and a tower, whose top reaches to the sky, and let's make us a name; lest we be scattered abroad on the surface of the whole earth." Yahveh came down to see the city and the tower, which the children of men built. Yahveh said, "Behold, they are one people, and they have all one language; and this is what they begin to do. Now nothing will be withheld from them, which they intend to do. Come, let's go down, and there confuse their language, that they may not understand one another's speech." So Yahveh scattered them abroad from there on the surface of all the earth. They stopped building the city. Therefore the name of it was called Babel because Yahveh confused the language of all the earth, there. From there, Yahveh scattered them abroad on the surface of all the earth."

—Genesis 11:1-9

This HAARP project bears a remarkable resemblance to the establishing of ancient Babel, the outcome of which was scattering and confusion. Could it be that this is the very thing that is bringing about the fall of the USA as a world empire? Quite possible as it is the very thing that brought about the fall of Lucifer who is known as Satan today:

> *"How you are fallen from heaven, day-star, son of the morning! How you are cut down to the ground, who laid the nations low! You said in your heart, I will ascend into heaven, I will exalt My throne above the stars of God; and I will sit on the mountain of congregation, in the uttermost parts of the north; I will ascend above the heights of the clouds; I will make myself like the Most High.* Yet you shall be brought down to Sheol, to the uttermost parts of the pit. Those who see you shall gaze at you, they shall consider you, [saying], "Is this the man who made the earth to tremble, who shook kingdoms; who made the world as a wilderness, and overthrew the cities of it; who didn't let loose his prisoners to their home?" All the kings of the nations, all of them, sleep in glory, everyone in his own house. But you are cast forth away from your tomb like an abominable branch, clothed with the slain, who are thrust through with the sword, who go down to the stones of the pit; as a dead body trodden under foot."
>
> —Isaiah 14:12-19

The fall of Lucifer was due to pride, the same pride that some world leaders have when they think that they can manipulate the creation for their own agendas! However, even this is part of the judgment of the Almighty. It is He who permits man to carry his pride to extremes and cause him to be trapped by the works of his own hands.

> Yahveh has made Himself known. He has executed judgment. The wicked is snared by the work of his own hands.
>
> —Psalm 9:16

According to this report the HAARP project has not yet been used to manipulate the weather, so all the hurricanes and tsunamis this year have happened without the intervention of man. This year we have had the most devastating storms in the history of the USA (Katrina) and in the history of the Far East (Asian tsunami).

But what could happen if or when the "superpowers" use the HAARP project? Would the world suffer at the hands of wicked men who would use the Almighty's creations at whim and for their own agendas? How would you like to be a citizen in a country that is a victim of the Big Boys playing God with their Big Toys such as the HAARP project?

But hasn't man played God from the beginning? And was it not Satan himself who deceived the Man and the Woman to do it? So is the HAARP project a surprise at all or rather the natural outcome of the sin of man who has risen to 'play God' from the beginning?

> "Now the serpent was more subtle than any animal of the field which Yahveh God had made. He said to the woman, "Yes, has God said, 'You shall not eat of any tree of the garden?'" The woman said to the serpent, "Of the fruit of the trees of the garden we may

eat, but of the fruit of the tree which is in the midst of the garden, God has said, 'You shall not eat of it, neither shall you touch it, lest you die.'" The serpent said to the woman, "You won't surely die, for God knows that in the day you eat it, your eyes will be opened, and you will be as God, knowing good and evil." When the woman saw that the tree was good for food, and that it was a delight to the eyes, and that the tree was to be desired to make one wise, she took of the fruit of it, and ate; and she gave some to her husband, and he ate. Both of their eyes were opened, and they knew that they were naked. They sewed fig leaves together, and made themselves aprons."

—Genesis 3:1-7

The wicked rulers of the earth who plan to manipulate winds (that Yah has created for Himself) in order to further their own perverted agendas have eaten of the forbidden tree and have tapped into some power resources that the Almighty Himself created. God Himself created the Tree of Knowledge, yet Adam tapped into this power resource *unauthorized!* *So have these wicked rulers have tapped into and are planning to use Yahveh's winds for their good pleasure! During the Second World War, the same thing happened. Wasn't Hitler the one who brought about the extermination of six million Jews - another one like the wicked rulers over the HAARP project? He played God in His time and through the channeling of evil spirits and dark forces brought all of*

Europe into devastation. Where is Hitler now? And where is the Third Reich Germany, that wanted to conquer the world? They are all gone, just like the Greek and Roman Empires of old. However, these big boys, with their big selfish ambitions, hurt the earth and its inhabitants greatly!

In the next chapters we will learn how to deal with the "Hitlers" of this present new world order and see which snake is stronger - The unauthorized abuse of knowledge and power or the authorized use of His mighty power. However, please remember that neither man, nor the devil can create anything at all. They can only tap into what Elohim has created, without His authority; like those thieves who tap into legal telephone and electric lines and use them for their own use. They did not establish those power lines and neither do they pay taxes to the city in order to use them. They just take their power AS IF they are legally entitled.

The wisest man that ever lived and the author of all winds and tempests said:

> "The thief only comes to steal, kill, and destroy. I came that they may have life, and may have it abundantly."
>
> —John 10:10

However, though the thieves, the wicked rulers and the magicians of this world are tapping illegally into God's knowledge, power and resources. It does not mean that the Almighty Himself is not using His own resources to bring about His judgment. After all, the snake of Moses (Aaron's rod representing Yahveh's authority) ate all the other snakes of the magicians that imitated the plagues in Egypt!

> "Yahveh spoke to Moses and to Aaron, saying, "When Pharaoh speaks to you, saying, 'Perform a miracle!' then you shall tell Aaron, 'Take your rod, and cast it down before Pharaoh, that it become a serpent.'" Moses and Aaron went in to Pharaoh, and they did so, as Yahveh had commanded: and Aaron cast down his rod before Pharaoh and before his servants, and it became a serpent. Then Pharaoh also called for the wise men and the sorcerers. They also, the magicians of Egypt, did in like manner with their enchantments. For they cast down every man his rod, and they became serpents: but Aaron's rod swallowed up their rods."
>
> —Exodus 7:8-12

So it will be in these End Times that the rod of judgment of the Most High will swallow the HAARP Project and all the manipulative rods of the wicked and prideful rulers of our time!

Let us remember that Stormy Weather has been occurring in the USA, Europe, Central America and the Far East more than ever and that this is a warning from the Almighty for two major reasons,

1. The way the nations are treating Israel by supporting terror against her and pushing her to give up biblical land and establish a Palestinian terrorist state..
2. For the idolatry, immorality and injustice of the nations. The earth is almost at the stage of Sodom and Gomorrah and it is desirous to vomit the sin out! Yahveh said,

"Because the cry of Sodom and Gomorrah is great, and because their sin is very grievous, I will go down now, and see whether they have done altogether according to the cry of it, which is come to Me. If not, I will know."

—Genesis 18:20-21

Though the HAARP project is the work of men inspired by Satan himself; still it is the Almighty Himself who has permitted this for His own end and for a certain day called, the day of evil or the day of judgment. When and if they choose to manipulate the weather, could it be that the Almighty will use it as a boomerang against the very nations that are trying to manipulate the weather? Those big boys with their big toys and their nations, can be seriously burned by trying to 'play God'. Lucifer did that and he experienced the 'Humpty Dumpty had a great fall' syndrome. The ancient King of Babylon tried that once and he ended up in the jungle eating grass for seven years... The question is how much more stormy weather are we to endure? And if there are a lot more storms ahead, are you sure that one of them will not catch up with you? Are you ready for what lies ahead?

The Noah Generation

> Will He destroy the earth through a flood like He did in the times of Noah? Yahveh saw that the wickedness of man was great in the earth, and that every imagination of the thoughts of his heart was only evil continually. Yahveh was sorry that He had made man on the earth, and it grieved Him in His heart. Yahveh said, "I will destroy man whom I have created from the surface of the ground; man, along with animals, creeping things, and birds of the sky; for I am sorry that I have made them."
>
> —Genesis 6:5-7

The same Yahveh is seeing the same thing today; the wickedness of man is great in the earth! Slave trade of women and children abounds, as does the murder of unborn babies, the love of mammon, which is the root of all evil, anti-Semitism and hatred of His Jewish people. There is abounding perversion and homosexuality, as in the days of Sodom and Gomorrah; man manipulating God's creation through genetic engineering, cloning and projects like the HAARP, witchcraft, satanic worship and satanic music, rebellion against parents, the perversion of calling both good and God evil and calling evil good, and the list of wickedness in the earth is endless...

One of the major sins that is incurring Elohim's judgment today, is the terrible ungodly and rebellious relationship between parents and their children! Most modern parents are no example of morality, righteousness and fear of God to their own children. And most children are disrespectful and rebellious towards parents. The boundary line between who is the parent and who is the child is unclear.

> "Remember you the law of Moses My servant, which I commanded to him in Horeb for all Israel, even statutes and ordinances. Behold, I will send you Elijah the prophet before the great and terrible day of Yahveh comes. He shall turn the heart of the fathers to the children, and the heart of the children to their fathers; lest I come and strike the earth with a curse."
> —Malachi 4:4-6

Because of the terrible and perverted relationship between ungodly parents and rebellious children, the earth is already suffering from a curse! But what does the law of Moses, the Torah say about this?

> "Honor your father and your mother, that your days may be long in the land which Yahveh your God gives you."
> —Exodus 20:12

This is the fifth of the top Ten Commandments! Is that therefore a surprise that so many children and young people are in mental hospitals, suffer from mental sickness and commit suicide, so their days are shortened? The earth is truly suffering from a curse.

> "But Noah found favor in Yahveh's eyes. This is the history of the generations of Noah. Noah was a righteous man, blameless among the people of his time. Noah walked with God."
>
> —Genesis 6:8,9

Are you walking with God like Noah in the midst of a perverted generation, or are you deceived into thinking that you are a god, yourself?

> "The earth was corrupt before God, and the earth was filled with violence. God saw the earth, and saw that it was corrupt, for all flesh had corrupted their way on the earth. God said to Noah, "The end of all flesh has come before Me, for the earth is filled with violence through them. Behold, I will destroy them with the earth."
>
> —Genesis 6:11-13

Is the earth corrupt now or does righteousness and good morals abound? I remember when I arrived in New Zealand. I was thinking to myself: What does this Jewish woman from a war-torn and oppressed country like Israel have to give to the people in New Zealand? They have a gorgeous, Garden of Eden of a country and they are at war with no one. No one is trying to take their land away and they are not hated for being "kiwis". Even the producers of the famous movie "The Lord of the Rings" agree with me! Right? Wrong! The moment I arrived in New Zealand and I opened the first newspaper comfortably sitting in one of Auckland's cafés, I saw the reason for my coming to New Zealand. These people are coming apart. They have the highest rate of teen pregnancy in the world, because they allow little girls to pervert their bodies at the early age of 15! Even France forbids fornication until the age of 16! Even France, the land of free sex! And New Zealand suffers from the highest rates of suicide worldwide! Why? Because no matter how many beautiful mountains and lakes you may have, when you break the laws of the Creator and forsake Him altogether, you suffer the consequences of emptiness, despair, depression...Yes and even suicide! Well, I said to myself, the devil seems to be running New Zealand, so this Jew from the war-torn, persecuted and rejected nation of Israel, which brought the world the Bible, the Holy Scriptures, has definitely got something to do here!

> "Yahveh said to Noah, "Come with all of your household into the ark, for I have seen your righteousness before Me in this generation. You shall take seven pairs of every clean animal with you, the male and his female. Of the animals that are not clean, take two, the male and his female. Also of the birds of the sky, seven and seven, male and female, to keep seed

> alive on the surface of all the earth. In seven days, I will cause it to rain on the earth for forty days and forty nights. Every living thing that I have made, I will destroy from the surface of the ground." Noah did everything that Yahveh commanded him. Noah was six hundred years old when the flood of waters came on the earth"
>
> —Genesis 7:1-6

Noah did everything that Yahveh commanded him, and he and his household were spared this terrible judgment! That is why you and I are alive today because of the obedience of that one righteous man before Yah!

The animals were wiser than men and many animals were rescued from the flood because of their obedience to Yahveh! How would you like to experience a tsunami or a hurricane where your cat or your dog makes it but you and your children drown because of your disobedience to the Almighty?

"It happened after the seven days, that the waters of the flood came on the earth.

> In the six hundredth year of Noah's life, in the second month, on the seventeenth day of the month, on the same day all the fountains of the great deep were burst open, and the sky's windows were opened. The rain was on the earth forty days and forty nights. In the same day Noah, and Shem, Ham, and Japheth,

the sons of Noah, and Noah's wife, and the three wives of his sons with them, entered into the ark; they, and every animal after its kind, all the cattle after their kind, every creeping thing that creeps on the earth after its kind, and every bird after its kind, every bird of every sort. They went to Noah into the ark, by pairs of all flesh with the breath of life in them. Those who went in, went in male and female of all flesh, as God commanded him; and Yahveh shut him in. The flood was forty days on the earth. The waters increased, and lifted up the ark, and it was lifted up above the earth."

—Genesis 7:10-17

For seven days the gates of Noah's Ark were open, in case some people would wake up, repent and join the wise crowd of a few people and many animals! But no more people came... Only the snail made it! Are we now during the period of 'seven days' or maybe seven years of grace, when the gates are open for you to be saved from the wrath to come? And maybe afterward *-Bam- the gates will close forever on* you?

Keep Reading, Don't Give Up!

The waters prevailed, and increased greatly on the earth, and the ark floated on the surface of the waters. The waters prevailed exceedingly on the earth. All the high mountains that were under the whole sky were covered. The waters prevailed fifteen cubits upward, and the mountains were covered. All flesh died that moved on the earth, including birds, cattle, animals, every creeping thing that creeps on the earth, and every man. All in whose nostrils was the breath of the spirit of life, of all that was on the dry land, died. Every living thing was destroyed that was on the surface of the ground, including man, cattle, creeping things, and birds of the sky. They were destroyed from the earth. Only Noah was left, and those who were with him in the ark."

—Genesis 7:18-23

Every living thing (outside of Noah's Ark) was destroyed! You and I owe our lives to Noah's obedience, and this righteous man is speaking to us again... There is a judgment coming, are you ready or will you perish?

However, do not think to yourselves that these terrible storms and tsunamis, as terrible and devastating as they have been, are the utmost of the judgment of Yah. No, no, no, these are like "pussy cats" because the Almighty, Elohim, the Creator, the Exalted One, promised to Noah that He would NEVER destroy the earth with a flood again. These floods and this Stormy Weather is only an introduction to God's judgment.

This time His judgment will be by *fire, so that those who reject Him and hate Him on the earth will have a taste of the eternal flames, which will accompany them in Hell forever!*

"Death and hades were thrown into the lake of fire. This is the second death, the lake of fire. If anyone was not found written in the book of life, he was cast into the lake of fire."

—Revelation 20:14,15

Are You Written in the Book of Life?

"And I will show wonders in the heavens and in the earth: blood, and fire, and pillars of smoke. The sun shall be turned into darkness, and the moon into blood, before the great and terrible day of Yahveh cometh. And it shall come to pass, that whosoever shall call on the name of Yahveh shall be delivered; for in mount Zion and in Jerusalem there shall be those who escape, as Jehovah hath said, and among the remnant those whom Yahveh doth call."

—Joel 2:30-32

Are you ready to call on His name or do you still trust your bank accounts, your presidents or your meteorologists?

"Therefore wait for Me," says Yahveh, "until the day that I rise up to the prey, for My determination is to gather the nations, that I may assemble the kingdoms, to pour on them My indignation, even all My fierce anger, for all the earth will be devoured with the fire of My jealousy.

For then I will purify the lips of the peoples that they may all call on the name of Yahveh, to serve

Him shoulder to shoulder. From beyond the rivers of Cush, My worshipers, even the daughter of My dispersed people, will bring My offering. In that day you will not be put to shame for all your doings, in which you have transgressed against Me; for then I will take away out of the midst of you your proudly exulting ones, and you will no more be haughty in My holy mountain. But I will leave in the midst of you an afflicted and poor people, and they will take refuge in the name of Yahveh"

—Zephaniah 3:8-12

"For behold, the day comes, it burns as a furnace; and all the proud, and all who work wickedness, shall be stubble; and the day that comes shall burn them up, says Yahveh of Hosts, that it shall leave them neither root nor branch. But to you who fear My name shall the Sun of righteousness arise with healing in its wings, and you shall go forth, and gambol as calves of the stall."

—Malachi 4:2

The God of Israel in His great love and compassion has given the world 2000 years to repent since He sent His best gift to His earth. He is very patient and has waited for a long time for all peoples to repent and turn to Him, but man as a whole has decided that He needs no Creator. Some think that it was man that invented God and others are a law unto themselves. They are so wicked as to device a project like the HAARP. Therefore He is warning us from Heaven saying - Time is UP! All those people in New Orleans who suffered from Katrina or those in Asia who suffered from the tsunami lost everything they had. Whatever you put your trust in besides the Almighty Himself can be lost in a second!

> "Yahveh has made everything for its own end - Yes, even the wicked (HAARP!) for the day of evil. Everyone who is proud in heart is an abomination to Yahveh: They shall assuredly not be unpunished. By mercy and truth iniquity is atoned for. By the fear of Yahveh men depart from evil."
> —Proverbs 16:3-6

> "You pronounced judgment from heaven. The earth feared, and was silent"
> —Psalm 76:8

Before we go on talking about Stormy Weather let us take a break and let me introduce you to my best friend and the one that will help us still all the storms and find what is truly valuable in life...

CHAPTER FIVE

The Man That Stills the Storms

"When he got into a boat, His disciples followed Him. Behold, a great tempest arose in the sea, so much that the boat was covered with the waves, but He was asleep. They came to Him, and woke Him up, saying, "Save us, Lord! We are dying!" He said to them, "Why are you fearful, oh you of little faith?" Then he got up, rebuked the wind and the sea, and there was a great calm. The men marveled, saying, "What kind of man is this, that even the wind and the sea obey Him?"
—Matthew 8:23-27

About 2,000 years ago a Man like none other was born of the people of Israel, of the tribe of Judah in the city of Bethlehem near Jerusalem.* He was born in a strange way fulfilling the prophecy given by the Prophet Isaiah to Israel by their God. The sign of the birth of the Savior-Messiah-Redeemer would be that a virgin woman would bear a child that would be termed Immanuel or God with us. This Immanuel child was named Yeshua, as He would be assigned to save His people, the Jews - then

* For more information about the divinity of Messiah, go into our website www.kad-esh.org and click "Teachings"

all those of the nations who would believe in Him and turn from their sins would be free from the eternal judgment that all mankind deserves for breaking The Commandments of the Creator.

> "Who has believed our message? And to whom has the arm of Yahveh been revealed? For He grew up before Him as a tender plant, and as a root out of a dry ground: He has no form nor comeliness; and when we see Him, there is no beauty that we should desire Him. He was despised, and rejected of men; a man of sorrows, and acquainted with grief: and as one from whom men hide their face He was despised; and we didn't respect Him."

For 2,000 years since He came, most peoples of the earth have disbelieved Him and have disrespected Him,

> "Surely He has borne our infirmities, and carried our sorrows; yet we esteemed him stricken, struck of God, and afflicted. But He was wounded for our transgressions, He was bruised for our iniquities; the chastisement of our peace was on Him; and with His stripes we are healed. All we like sheep have gone

astray; we have turned everyone to His own way, and Yahveh has laid on Him the iniquity of us all."

We have all been mistaken and have lost our way. Both Jews and Gentiles! Most people have mocked Him and used His name in vain as a cuss word:

"He was oppressed, yet when He was afflicted He didn't open His mouth, as a lamb that is led to the slaughter, and as a sheep that before its shearer is mute, so He didn't open His mouth. By oppression and judgment He was taken away, and as for His generation, who [among them] considered that He was cut off out of the land of the living for the disobedience of my people to whom the stroke [was due]?"

He suffered terribly because of *our disobedience! Not His!*

"They made His grave with the wicked, and with a rich man in His death, although He had done no violence, neither was any deceit in His mouth. Yet it pleased Yahveh to bruise Him, He has put him to grief: when you shall make His soul an offering for sin, He shall see [His] seed, He shall prolong His days, and the pleasure of Yahveh shall prosper in His hand. He shall see of the travail of His soul, [and] shall be satisfied: by the knowledge of Himself shall my righteous servant justify many, and He shall bear their iniquities."

—Isaiah 53

He had no sin. He committed no crime. His soul and body were the sacrifices and the offering for our sin! He Himself took the punishment that we deserve and paid the price that we may be forgiven by His father Yahveh, whose commandments we have all broken!

This Holy Man/Child/Messiah/King went about all of Israel doing good, teaching His father's word - the law given to Moses on Mount Sinai - with great authority. He healed the sick, cast out devils, fed the hungry and performed many miracles. Finally, without any guilt He was put to death by the Romans on an execution stake upon a hill east of Jerusalem, having been delivered into their hands by the religious leaders of the time who did not recognize Him as the awaited Messiah. He remained only three days in the grave and then to the astonishment of all, He rose from the dead, in a glorified body. Five hundred people saw Him after His resurrection. He remained with His Jewish disciples for 40 days and then gave them the charge to GO into the entire world and tell them they need to be saved from the wrath to come. He then ascended to Heaven awaiting the time of His return as a conquering King to Jerusalem, Israel; thus fulfilling the prophecies in the Book of Zechariah 12 and 14. In Israel we have many ancient tombs, including the tomb of Abraham, Isaac and Jacob in Hebron. The bones of these ancient patriarchs are still there, however, the tomb of Yeshua, the Holy Messiah, is empty because He is *risen*.

Those who would put their trust in this Jewish risen Man (who died to take upon Himself the punishment that we deserved for breaking His father's Commandments), would have their sins forgiven and their lives transformed to follow Him and to obey His father's (the God of Israel also called Yahveh) Commandments.

Those of Jerusalem and Israel who believed in Him after His Resurrection became the disciples of old who worked tremendous miracles in His Name. They became the church fathers and the true founders of His Body of Believers. Those of the Jews who did not believe in Him were exiled out of their God-given Land and have suffered at the hands of the Gentiles and most particularly the Christians for nearly 2000 years. For 2000 years the father in heaven has extended much grace to the nations through His Holy Son Yeshua. For 2000 years the nations at large have rejected Him as a Jew and have created a Greek savior of their own, killing also His offspring the Jewish people and following other gods which are no gods at all.

This book has been written as an act of grace to the nations so that they will wake up to the fact that Yahveh is about to judge the world for rejecting His Son, whom He sent, and for rejecting His ways and Holy Commandments, for rejecting His people Israel - the Jewish people, and for dividing their land.

"The devil who deceived them was thrown into the lake of fire and sulfur, where are also the beast and the false prophet. They will be tormented day and night forever and ever. I saw a great white throne, and Him who sat on it, from whose face the earth and the heaven fled away. There was found no place for them. I saw the dead, the great and the small, standing before the throne. Books were opened. Another book was opened, which is the book of life. The dead were judged out of the things that were written in the books, according to their works. The sea gave up the dead which were in it. Death and Hades gave up the dead who were in them. They were judged, each one according to his works. Death and Hades were thrown into the lake of fire. This is the second death, the lake of fire. If anyone was not found written in the book of life, was cast into the lake of fire."

—Revelation 20:10-15

This book is also written to ask His people Israel for forgiveness on behalf of the church for misrepresenting the Messiah for so long, and hurting the Jewish people terribly through that. May the Almighty give you a heart of forgiveness for so many years of pain at the hands of deceived Christians who persecuted you through pogroms, Inquisitions and the Holocaust.

As a Jew I also want to provoke you, my Jewish people to repent for rejecting Yeshua for so long and exchanging Him for false messiahs of your own making and to be restored to the father in heaven through the Son whom He sent. There is salvation in no other name or Messiah, but in the name of Yeshua alone. He is the Word, the law, the Torah made flesh and is the only One who can save us from eternal judgment and from the wrath to come. He is the One who will rule and reign from the Holy Temple in Jerusalem very soon.

> "I will pour on the house of David, and on the inhabitants of Jerusalem, the spirit of grace and of supplication, and they shall look to me whom they have pierced, and they shall mourn for Him, as one mourns for His only son, and shall be in bitterness for Him, as one who is in bitterness for his firstborn."
> —Zechariah 12:10

This is also a call to those who have been mistaken in their 'political views' about Israel and have sided with the establishment of a Palestinian state, or have even have hated the Jews and Israel altogether. For whoever comes against Israel, His chosen people, whom the Almighty is preparing for the return of His holy son, King and Messiah to earth, shall be severely judged.

> "And in that day will I make Jerusalem a burdensome stone for all people: all that burden themselves with it shall be cut in pieces, though all the people of the earth be gathered together against it."
> —Zechariah 12:3

You can be saved from the wrath of the Creator in spite of your ungodly, rebellious and defiant ways - by believing, trusting and obeying His Holy Son, Yeshua, the Jewish Messiah:

> "For God so loved the world, that He gave His one and only Son, that whoever believes in Him should not perish, but have eternal life." For God didn't send His Son into the world to judge the world, but that the world should be saved through him. He who believes in Him is not judged. He who doesn't believe has been judged already because he has not believed in the name of the only born son of God. This is the judgment, that the light has come into the world, and men loved the darkness rather than the light, for their works were evil. For everyone who does evil hates the light, and doesn't come to the light, for fear that His works would be reproved. But he who does the truth comes to the light, that His works may be revealed, that they have been done with God."
>
> —John 3:16-21

The time for the nations to be saved from God's judgment is coming to an end. The Almighty has had patience with the nations for 2,000 years!

> "For I don't desire, brothers, to have you ignorant of this mystery, so that you won't be wise in your own conceits, that a hardening in part has happened to

Israel until the fullness of the Gentiles have come in, and so all Israel will be saved. Even as it is written, "There will come out of Zion the Deliverer, And He will turn away ungodliness from Jacob. This is my covenant to them, when I will take away their sins." Concerning the gospel, they are enemies for your sake. But concerning the election, they are beloved for the fathers` sake. For the gifts and the calling of God are irrevocable."

—Romans 11:25-29

Whoever you may be, Jewish, Christian, Moslem, Buddhist, Hindu, New Age or Atheist, this might be your last opportunity to believe in, accept and follow this Jewish Messiah. Maybe in a few seconds a tsunami or a hurricane will come your way. But more dangerous than that is the hell that really exists and it is a place of constant burning and torment - which is reserved for those who choose to reject the amazing love of God, manifested in the person of Yeshua the Jewish Messiah. They will spend eternity (an amazingly long time) separated from life, love, goodness and mercy - suffering terribly, forever.

> "For as in those days which were before the flood they were eating and drinking, marrying and giving in marriage, until the day that Noah entered into the ark, and they didn't know until the flood came, and took them all away, so will be the coming of the Son

of Man. Then will two men be in the field: one is taken, and one is left."

—Matthew 24:38-40

Repent, return and submit to the Creator who loved you so much and sent His Son to take the punishment - that you deserve for breaking God's eternal Commandments as given to Moses the deliverer of Israel. Then, even in the midst of the storms, He will be with you, He will quiet you with His love and give you peace and a sense of well-being, a Shalom that you have never experienced. Even more so, *He will give you power and authority over sin and devils and life in His Presence forever!*

Bend your knees and pray with me:

Dear father in heaven, Holy God of Israel, I am lost without You. Please forgive me for going my own way and for rejecting Your holy son Yeshua for so long. I receive Him now as my savior, master and king and I forsake all other masters. I renounce my unbelief and disobedience to You. From now on I am Yours, please forgive me, change me and help me to follow You forever - so I can be saved from Your judgment. Please write Your laws and Commandments in my heart so I can obey You. Fill me with Your spirit of holiness and with Your presence. I pray in the name of the one that gave His life for me and took my punishment that I can live as Your child forever. In Yeshua's name, amen.

If you prayed this prayer from your heart, congratulations! You have passed from death to life! As you read this book you will be prepared for the Stormy Weather ahead of us! Please contact us and tell us of your decision so we can pray for you and help you to walk this road. You can order my book, "Grafted In", online which will help you and instruct you, www.kad-esh.org, info@kad-esh.org

> "Enter in by the narrow gate; for wide is the gate, and broad is the way, that leads to destruction, and many are those who enter in by it. How narrow is the gate, and restricted is the way that leads to life! Few are those who find it."
>
> —Matthew 7:13,14

And now let us resume our discussion on how to prepare for this Stormy Weather that is ahead of us.

CHAPTER SIX
Are There Angels in the Storms?

"He makes His messengers winds;
His servants flames of fire."
—Psalm 104:4

In Hebrew the word for "winds" is the same word for spirit, *ruach* (singular); *ruchot* (plural). So winds are likened unto spiritual entities and they are created to be servants of the Creator or messengers, or in Hebrew, angels or *malachim*.

So, let us paraphrase this Scripture directly from the original Hebrew Scriptures:

He makes His Angels like *winds* or *spirits*.

There is a direct correlation between the spiritual realm and the behavior of winds. When Yah sends winds of judgment, it is His angels of judgment and destruction that He sends. As we mentioned previously, He sent His Angel to destroy the first-born sons of all of Egypt, to judge Israel at the time of King David.

There are other times however, when Satan, the chief fallen angel originally named Lucifer, sends those angels that fell with him to create contrary winds and storms and those are demonic winds:

> "There was war in the sky. Michael and his angels made war on the dragon. The dragon and his angels made war. They didn't prevail, neither was a place found for him anymore in heaven. The great dragon was thrown down, the old serpent, he who is called the devil and Satan, the deceiver of the whole world. He was thrown down to the earth, and his angels were thrown down with him."
>
> —Revelation 12:7-9

We see that Lucifer fell from Heaven because of pride as we mentioned in Chapter Four of this book. But we also see that some angels called 'his angels' or 'Satan's angels' (created by God!) fell with him. Those angels are Satan's army which comes to steal, kill and destroy on the earth. Satan's angels, though created by Elohim, are cooperating with Satan's hidden agenda and with projects such as the HAARP project.

Fallen Angels in the Winds

And behold, there arose a great tempest in the sea, insomuch that the boat was covered with the waves: but He was asleep. And they came to Him, and awoke Him, saying Save, Lord; we perish. And He saith unto them, Why are ye fearful, O ye of little faith? Then He arose, and rebuked the winds and the sea, and there was a great calm. And the men marveled, saying, What manner of man is this, that even the winds and the sea obey Him?

—Matthew 8:24-26

When we read this passage it can make us wonder why Yeshua rebuked the winds if it was His father, the one that sends them, to do His will? The answer is very simple - There were fallen angels, unclean spirits in that storm. Remember that some of the angels left with Lucifer, who is Satan? Those are also winds (ruchot) or spirits, but they are demonic spirits who were trying to kill Yeshua and His disciples through unleashing a violent storm. That is why the master rebuked them because they were not doing the father's will.

A true man or woman of God has the authority over these contrary demonic winds and spirits, that cause unauthorized storms!

There was another instance when those same spirits tried to hinder Peter,

> And in the fourth watch of the night He came unto them, walking upon the sea. And when the disciples saw Him walking on the sea, they were troubled, saying, It is a ghost, and they cried out for fear. But straightway Yeshua spoke unto them, saying Be of good cheer; it is I; be not afraid. And Peter answered Him and said, Lord, if it be thou, bid me come unto thee upon the waters. And He said, Come. And Peter went down from the boat and walked upon

the waters to come to Yeshua. But when He saw the wind, He was afraid; and beginning to sink, He cried out, saying, Lord, save me. And immediately Yeshua stretched forth His hand, and took hold of him, and saith unto him, O thou of little faith, wherefore didst thou doubt?

—Matthew 14:25-31

Peter was already doing the impossible by obeying the master and walking on the water. No man besides Yeshua had ever done that before! This was new territory for Peter who was trying his faith. Then those winds began to blow for the purpose of frightening him and hindering him as a Man of Faith. Instead of Peter rebuking those winds and recognizing the activity of evil spirits, He 'looked at them' in fear. Once the spirit of fear entered him, He began to sink.

We should never "look into the eyes" of contrary winds and hindering spirits but we should simply take authority over them and rebuke them. Any holy child of God who is walking in obedience to Yeshua has the authority to stop all unauthorized storms. The key factor is "Walking in obedience to Yeshua - that is a holy walk".

And He called unto him his twelve disciples, and gave them authority over unclean spirits, to cast them out, and to heal all manner of disease and all manner of sickness.

—Matthew 10:1

If you are a true disciple of the master you also have power over unclean spirits or unauthorized winds! Disciples are those who are instructed and corrected so that they can learn to walk in the footsteps of their master. True disciples are trained in obedience to His Commandments!

One of our team members who had backslidden prior to coming to work with us came to us in a much-compromised state. I did not know when I allowed her to come that she had not been walking in holiness, however, the Holy Spirit impressed me to receive her. In less than two months with us, she had been thoroughly transformed and was walking in holiness and righteousness. She had become a disciple and was willing to be instructed and corrected to learn obedience.

In one of our training sessions, we were ministering deliverance to our group. I needed more laborers so I asked this particular team member if she had ever cast out demons before. She immediately reacted in fear and said, "nnnooo". In other words she did not want to do it because she had never done it before! But as she was now walking in holiness having become a disciple, I told her she would minister today and just do what I do. Needless to say, she was soon casting out devil after devil and enjoying every minute of it! This was especially when she saw the awesome result of her labors in the people whom she ministered to. Every true disciple of Yeshua is called to exercise authority over unclean spirits and to stop their illegal work on the earth!

Behold, I have given you authority to tread upon serpents and scorpions, and over all the power of the enemy: and nothing shall in any wise hurt you. Nevertheless, in this rejoice not, that the spirits are subject unto you; but rejoice that your names are written in heaven.

—Luke 10:19-20

And these signs shall accompany them that believe: in my name shall they cast out demons; they shall speak with new tongues, they shall take up serpents, and if they drink any deadly thing, it shall in no wise hurt them; they shall lay hands on the sick, and they shall recover.

—Mark 16:17,18

The Obedient Heavenly Army

The other angels that did not fall and remained faithful to Elohim we will call - the obedient heavenly army or host. These will not be manipulated by man or Satan and will do Yah's will only. These are at the service of the obedient people of Yahveh!

Let us get acquainted with them:

"Aren't they all ministering spirits, sent forth to do service for the sake of those who will inherit salvation?"

—Hebrews 1:14

They are servants to those that believe in Yeshua. The word for salvation in Hebrew is Yeshuá,

> "Praise Yahveh, you angels of His, Who are mighty in strength, who fulfill His word, Obeying the voice of His word."
>
> —Psalm 103:20

1. They are mighty in strength.
2. They fulfill Yah's Word and bring it to pass
3. They obey the voice (sound) of His Word
4. They are His messengers (malach in Hebrew means angel, messenger, sent out one)

In other words, Elohim's obedient heavenly army or a host of angels are there to do Yah's will by serving those who are His children, bringing His word to come to pass and going wherever or doing whatever they hear God tell them to do. These awesome angels who are mighty in strength are no little 'babies with wings' as many mistaken artists depict them. No, they are not little cute naked babies flying around. These are awesome, fearsome messengers and warriors of the Most High who execute *all of His orders and they do not retreat until they have done it. These awesome beings work together with those who follow Yeshua and serve* them!

Two of these holy angels were sent to destroy Sodom and Gomorrah and to rescue Lot, Abraham's nephew:

> "Two angels came to Sodom at evening. Lot sat in the gate of Sodom. Lot saw them and rose up to

meet them. He bowed himself with his face to the earth, and He said: "See now, my lords, please turn aside into your servant's house, stay all night, wash your feet, and you will rise up early, and go on your way." They said, "No, but we will stay in the street all night." He urged them greatly, and they came in with him and entered into his house. He made them a feast, and baked unleavened bread, and they ate."

—Genesis 19:1-3

We can see that His angels look like men, though they are messenger spirits. They ate Lot's food as any man would eat.

But before they lay down, the men of the city, the men of Sodom, surrounded the house, both young and old, all the people from every quarter. "They called to Lot, and said to him, "Where are the men who came into you this night? Bring them out to us, that we may have sex with them." Lot went out to them to the door and shut the door after him. He said: "Please, my brothers, don't act so wickedly. See now, I have two virgin daughters. Please let me bring them out to you, and do you to them as is good in your eyes. Only don't do anything to these men because they have come under the shadow of my roof." They said: "Stand back! This one fellow came into sojourn, and he appoints himself a judge. Now will we deal worse with you, than with them!" They

pressed hard on the man, even Lot, and drew near to break the door. But the men put forth their hand, and brought Lot into the house to them, and shut the door. They struck the men who were at the door of the house with blindness, both small and great, so that they wearied themselves to find the door."
—Genesis 19:4-11

They have the power and authority to harm, blind or kill wicked men who oppose God's will. They are endowed with supernatural strength and powers.

"The men said to Lot, "Do you have anybody else here? Your son-in-law, your sons, your daughters, and whomever you have in the city, bring them out of the place: for we will destroy this place because the cry of them is grown great before Yahveh. Yahveh has sent us to destroy it."
—Genesis 19:12,13

They can rescue the righteous and the covenant people and they can destroy entire cities!

"It came to pass when they had taken them out, that He said, "Escape for your life! Don't look behind you, neither stay anywhere in the plain. Escape to the mountain, lest you be consumed!"
—Genesis 19:17

They serve us but they also give us instruction.

> "Then Yahveh rained on Sodom and on Gomorrah sulfur and fire from Yahveh out of the sky. He overthrew those cities, all the plain, all the inhabitants of the cities, and that which grew on the ground. But his wife looked back from behind him, and she became a pillar of salt."
>
> —Genesis 19:24-26

Lot's wife foolishly took the instruction of these holy angels lightly and suffered the consequences! Until this day she decorates the desert of Israel as a pillar of salt.

Having thus been acquainted with the ministry of these awesome and fearsome spirit messengers, let us see their involvement in storms and weather:

> "When He opened the seventh seal, there followed a silence in heaven for about half an hour. I saw the seven angels who stand before God, and seven trumpets were given to them. Another angel came and stood over the altar, having a golden censer. Much incense was given to Him, that He should add it to the prayers of all the saints on the golden altar, which was before the throne. The smoke of the incense, with the prayers of the saints, went up before God out of the angel's hand. The angel took the censer, and He filled it with the fire of the altar and threw

it on the earth. There followed thunders, sounds, lightning, and an earthquake."

—Revelation 8:1-5

Here we see that the angel assists the saints (the believers and disciples of Messiah) in their prayers by adding incense and then by throwing the prayers of the saints on the earth thus creating a terrible weather problem that includes an earthquake and a thunderstorm! We can see a real close cooperation here between this particular angel and the praying saints. Could it be that some of our prayers are causing earthquakes and storms?

An Earthquake in Peru

We were in Peru during the year 2005, establishing a new work. Prior to the special meeting of dedication of the leaders of this work, Rabbi Baruch, Rev. Daniel my armor-bearer, Pastor Anita the designated pastor for this new work and I, were 'praying up a storm' in my room that was on the second story of the ministry house. I was crying out before Yah about the condition of Peru and of the church there and for their need to be restored to the original apostolic Jewish roots of the faith. I reminded Yah of His promise which He gave me when I was consecrated to be a Bishop in London:

> "Oh that you would tear the heavens, that you would come down, that the mountains might quake at your presence, as when fire kindles the brushwood, [and] the fire causes the waters to boil; to make your name

known to your adversaries, that the nations may tremble at your presence! When you did terrible things which we didn't look for, you came down, the mountains quaked at your presence. For from of old men have not heard, nor perceived by the ear, neither has the eye seen a God besides you, who works for Him who waits for him."

—Isaiah 64:1-4

So, I was praying fervently for His Presence to come down on Lima, Peru, the city that used to be one of the major seats of the Inquisition in times past and that killed so many people. There is a sign in the Lima Inquisition Museum that says that over 80% of those killed by the Inquisition there were Jews!

So, we prayed earnestly for Yah to rend the heavens and come down. We prayed for His presence to shake this nation and bring it to its knees and for our new MAP (Messianic Apostolic Prophetic) work in Lima to be impacting and relevant; to really make a difference. When we finished this strong prayer, we were spent! We came down to where all were waiting for us and their first question was:

Did you feel the earthquake? We said, "No, we were praying too hard. What earthquake?" All of Lima, Peru had been hit with a 5.0 on the Richter scale earthquake. Everyone felt it, the radio was talking about it, houses were shaken, but we felt nothing as we were too busy making it happen!

Shofars & Angels

"The seven angels who had the seven trumpets prepared themselves to sound. The first sounded, and there followed hail and fire, mingled with blood, and they were thrown on the earth. One third of the earth was burnt up, and one third of the trees were burnt up, and all green grass was burnt up. The second angel sounded, and something like a great mountain burning with fire was thrown into the sea. One third of the sea became blood, and one third of the creatures that were in the sea died, those who had life. One third of the ships were destroyed. The third angel sounded, and a great star fell from the sky, burning like a torch, and it fell on one third of the rivers, and on the springs of the waters. The name of the star is called "Wormwood." One third of the waters became wormwood. Many men died from the waters, because they were made bitter. The fourth angel sounded, and one third of the sun was struck, and one third of the moon, and one third of the stars, so that one third of them would be darkened, and the day wouldn't shine for one third of it, and the night in the same way. I saw, and I heard an eagle, flying in mid heaven, saying with a loud voice, "Woe! Woe! Woe for those who dwell on the earth, because of the other voices of the trumpets of the three angels, who are yet to sound."

—Revelation 8:6-13

Here we can see angels who sound trumpets and the outcome. I have experienced quite a bit with the sound of the trumpet and especially the shofar or the biblical horn. Four years before this earthquake we were in Peru again and went to visit the catacombs under the main Catholic Cathedral. There were thousands of bones under there of those slain during the Spanish/Peruvian Inquisition. It looks like the valley of the dry bones in the book of Ezekiel. I blew the shofar over those bones, calling the Sephardic (Spanish) Jews back to life and decreed Ezekiel 37 over those dead bones. This was the 31st of December 2001 and we had been in Lima for only 24 hours! It was a whirlwind visit. We left that evening before the New Year celebrations would begin. As we were flying off news came to us that there had been a great fire near the Museum of the Inquisition and the 'dead bones catacombs' and that many people died in that fire.

I was shocked. What had this shofar blowing over dead bones done? Later on, I heard that because of this terrible fire (that killed around 600 people!) the city hall forbade the traditional ceremonies of the 31st of December from taking place anymore! What were these traditional ceremonies which have been prevalent in almost every Latin American country and in Spain too? They were the burning of large paper dolls representing the old year. However, this is reminiscent of the Spanish Inquisition when they used to burn Jews in the bonfires for the simple crime of being Jewish! Later on, when they ran out of Jews to burn, they used paper dolls with a beard and a kippa (Jewish religious hat) and they would decree the words from 'the good old times' - "Burn Jew, burn to the bone, as for your sin (of killing Christ) even hell is not sufficient" In Peru, as in many other nations, they have continued with this demonic anti-Jewish ceremony. However, instead of calling it the Jew or Judas as they used to, they called it 'the old year'. They continued this practice until we blew the shofar, that is - the angel of Yahveh and I. Today that ceremony is totally forbidden in Lima, Peru. Did I know what my shofar blast was going to do? Did I want people to die? Of course not! But Yah had sent me to Peru in order to judge that demonic principality that had been ruling there for nearly 500 years, since the Spanish-Peruvian Inquisition!

I was not aware then, of the great impact of blowing the shofar under the apostolic prophetic anointing, and most particularly, my shofar. I could tell you a few stories of the impact that the sound of my shofar has had on entire nations and even continents. Sometimes it has brought tremendous breakthroughs like in the economy of Argentina. (That particular story appears in my book "Sheep Nations"). Another time it had great impact among the Aborigines in Australia, so the gospel could penetrate and advance. At other times it has caused political changes in Israel or in the USA. Suffice to say that the holy angels work with the anointed shofar blowers who are sent by Yah. Those same angels helped Joshua. After the Levites had blown their shofars the walls of Jericho came down and the city was conquered! Shofars are instruments of the spirit as they are instruments through which the wind (ruach) of the Holy Spirit and the holy angels, are both summoned and released. This is only when they are blown by a sanctified servant of the Most High, as in my case or the case of the Levites in Jericho.

> "So the people shouted, and [the priests] blew the trumpets, and it happened, when the people heard the sound of the trumpet, that the people shouted with a great shout, and the wall fell down flat, so that the people went up into the city, every man straight before him, and they took the city."
> —Joshua 6:20

Only the work of angels can cause a wall to fall down flat (like swallowed by the earth). There are some ruins of that in the Jericho archeological site in Israel, that shows the remains of the most ancient walled city in the world ever found!

"We can thus see that there is a close cooperation between Yah's servants and His holy angels. As you can see, the result of this cooperation is not always 'nice'. Sometimes it brings breakthrough and blessing and sometimes it brings breakthrough and judgment. Whatever the Almighty's will is in any given situation, His holy angels are mighty and they are there to make His Word come to pass - all of His will - and that includes Stormy Weather in times of judgment.

Then the earth shook and trembled. The foundations also of the mountains quaked and were shaken, because He was angry. There went up a smoke out of His nostrils, Fire out of His mouth devoured; coals were kindled by it. He bowed the heavens also and came down. Thick darkness was under His feet. He rode on a cherub and flew. Yes, He soared on the wings of the wind. He made darkness His hiding-place, His pavilion around him, darkness of waters, thick clouds of the skies. At the brightness before Him, his thick clouds passed, hailstones and coals of fire. Yahveh also thundered in the sky, the Most High uttered His voice, hailstones and coals of fire. He sent out His arrows, and scattered them; Yes, lightning manifold, and routed them. Then the channels of waters appeared, the foundations of the world were laid bare, at your rebuke, Yahveh, at the blast of the breath of your nostrils. (tsunami!) He sent from on high. He took me. He drew me out of many waters. He delivered me from my strong enemy, from those who hated me, for they were too mighty for me. They came on me on the day of my calamity, but Yahveh was my support. He brought me forth also into a large place. He delivered me because He delighted in me. Yahveh has rewarded me according to my righteousness. According to the cleanness of my hands has He recompensed me. For I have kept the ways of Yahveh, and have not wickedly departed from my God." Psalm 18:7-21

The Obedience Factor

Here we can see Yahveh Himself riding on a cherub on the wings of the winds and creating a tremendous storm in His anger against the wicked. He comes to judge the world. Though others who have no covenant protection from Him may be dying in this tempest, He rescues His covenant children who obey Him. He draws them out of many waters (a tsunami or a 'Katrina'). However, apart from the fact that the purpose of this terrible tempest is to come and judge in His fury, we can also see that in King David's case, he enjoyed special protection in the midst of a storm because of his obedience to the Commandments, statutes and ordinances of the Most High, just like in the case of Noah.

Obedience is a very important factor when it comes to Yah's covering of protection, in fact, the *most important* factor! Notice that the Almighty comes riding on a cherub, which is a very special type of angel; it is an angel of glory that remains in the presence of Yahveh! Could it be that He rode on the cherubs when He baptized the Jewish apostles in the Holy Spirit and fire on the day of Shavuot (Pentecost)? And is there any connection between their obedience and their empowerment?

1. They were obeying the master who told them to wait in Jerusalem for this empowerment. (Acts 1:4)
2. They were keeping the Commandment of one of the three pilgrim feasts when it was mandatory to come to Jerusalem and be in the presence of Yah (the holy

convocation of Shavuot - the feast of weeks. Leviticus 23)

3. They were in one accord. (Psalm 133)

"Now when the day of Pentecost had come, they were all with one accord in one place. Suddenly there came from the sky a sound like the rushing of a mighty wind, and it filled all the house where they were sitting. Tongues like fire appeared and were distributed to them, and it sat on each one of them. They were all filled with the Holy Spirit and began to speak with other languages, as the Spirit gave them the ability to speak."

—Acts 2:1-4

Here we meet a mighty wind. In other words, the moving throne of Yahveh made His dramatic entrance into that upper room in Jerusalem! The glory of Yahveh flew on His cherubim and His spirit, His ruach, His ultimate wind filled them all up! What a glorious moment!

"When the cherubim went, the wheels went beside them; and when the cherubim lifted up their wings to mount up from the earth, the wheels also didn't turn from beside them. When they stood, these stood; and when they mounted up, these mounted up with them: for the spirit of the living creature was in them. The glory of Yahveh went forth from over the threshold of the house, and stood over the cherubim."

—Ezekiel 10:16-18

I still remember that same glorious moment in my own life when after repenting from my sins and accepting Yeshua as my Messiah, savior and master, I also began to obey His Commandments! He commanded me to burn a picture of a witchcraft object that I had made when I was seeking for Him in the wrong places. As I burnt the picture of that Ouija board, the same mighty rushing wind came down from heaven upon me like a pressure shower of water, fire and wind and put me on my knees for five hours praying in all kinds of tongues. I had been baptized in the ruach (spirit) of His Holiness and I was never the same again. I had been *empowered* by His glorious presence!

Since then, both the power of His spirit and the evidence of the ministry of His holy angels have been very clear in my life! Wherever His presence and glory is, you will also find His obedient heavenly host. Every spirit baptized child of God should be empowered to work with the angels. It is through that empowerment that most signs, wonders and miracles happen and it was the glorious presence of abba's (father's) ruach (spirit) and malachim (angels) that was common during the early church time in Jerusalem. But also obedience to the Commandments of Yah was common then!

Judgment & Revival

"Elijah the Tishbite, who was of the sojourners of Gilead, said to Ahab: As Yahveh, the God of Israel, lives, before whom I stand, there shall not be dew nor rain these years, but according to my word. The word of Yahveh came to him, saying, Get you hence, and turn you eastward, and hide yourself by the brook Cherith, that is before the Jordan. It shall be, that you shall drink of the brook; and I have commanded the ravens to feed you there. So he went and did according to the word of Yahveh; for he went and lived by the brook Cherith, that is before the Jordan. The ravens brought him bread and flesh in the morning, and bread and flesh in the evening; and he drank of the brook."

—1 Kings 17:1-6

Elijah the Tishbite was Yah's prophet in the Northern Kingdom of Israel during the reign of wicked King Ahab and his witch of a wife Jezebel. They had perverted all of Israel with gross immorality and idolatry. The Prophet was sorely vexed by the sin of his people and he pronounced Yah's judgment over the land. The true prophets of the Most High have authority to pronounce judgment or blessing over entire areas. In this case we can see that judgment was executed through withholding the rain. Without rain, crops fail and cattle die and then the people suffer from famine. Famines are always signs of Yah's judgment. Eventually, in the third year of this terrible financial breakdown and economic collapse, Elijah confronted the king, the false prophets of Baal and Ashera (Ishtar), on Mount Carmel and displayed God's power before all of them - who ended up dead by Elijah's hand, inside of the brook Kishon. Needless to say, all of Israel then repented from idolatry. Only then did Elijah release rain on the earth and he did so by his prophetic declaration and his intercession.

> "Elijah said to Ahab, Get you up, eat and drink; for there is the sound of abundance of rain. So Ahab went up to eat and to drink. Elijah went up to the top of Carmel, and he bowed himself down on the earth, and put his face between his knees. He said to his servant, Go up now, look toward the sea. He went up, and looked, and said, There is nothing. He said, Go again seven times. It happened at the seventh time, that he said, Behold, there arises a cloud out of the sea, as small as a man's hand. He said, Go up, tell Ahab, Make ready [your chariot], and get you down, that the rain not stop you. It happened in a little while, that the sky grew black with clouds and wind, and there was a great rain. Ahab rode, and went to Jezreel: and the hand of Yahveh was on Elijah, and he girded up his loins, and ran before Ahab to the entrance of Jezreel."
>
> —1 Kings 18:41-46

When the prophet spoke the words that released the rain, the holy angels went into action to fulfill this word because Yah's Prophets are assigned to speak the words of the Most High. When Elijah went on top of Mount Carmel, he went to pray in order to release the angel that serves at the golden altar of Heaven, who adds incense to his prayers and pours out Elijah's prayers on the earth - which in turn caused winds and storm. In this case this was a welcome storm after a long drought.

> "Confess your offenses one to another, and pray one for another, that you may be healed. The effective, earnest prayer of a righteous man is powerfully effective. Elijah was a man with a nature like ours, and he prayed earnestly that it might not rain, and it didn't rain on the earth for three years and six months. He prayed again, and the sky gave rain, and the earth brought forth its fruit"
>
> —Yaakov (James) 5:16-18

The righteous people of Yahveh have power in their prayers to affect the entire planet and to activate Yah's holy angels. Probably most of the stormy weather that we have been experiencing these past years is connected with the earnest prayers of those saints who are crying out for revival and righteousness. Many of them have been blowing the shofars all over the earth, declaring a mighty move of Yah's spirit. By now the holy angels have been released to bring those prayers and prophetic words to pass - except when revival and judgment are intricately related. Elijah did not release the rain until he judged the prophets of Baal and Ashera in front of the people. Only after the public blood bath of these wicked priests who were corrupting Yah's people, did he prophesy rain and release it through intercession that in turn released angelic intervention.

> Elijah took twelve stones, according to the number of the tribes of the sons of Jacob, to whom the word of Yahveh came, saying, Israel shall be your name. With the stones he built an altar in the name of Yahveh; and he made a trench about the altar, as great as would contain two measures of seed. He put the wood in order, and cut the bull in pieces, and laid it on the wood. He said, Fill four jars with water, and pour it on the burnt offering, and on the wood. He said, Do it the second time; and they did it the second time. He said, Do it the third time; and they did it the third time. The water ran round about the altar; and he filled the trench also with water. It happened at the time of the offering of the [evening] offering, that Elijah the prophet came near, and said, Yahveh, the God of Abraham, of Isaac, and of Israel, let it be known this day that you are God in Israel, and that I am your servant, and that I have done all these things at your word. Hear me, Yahveh, hear me, that these people may know that you, Yahveh, are God,

and [that] you have turned their heart back again. Then the fire of Yahveh fell, and consumed the burnt offering, and the wood, and the stones, and the dust, and licked up the water that was in the trench. When all the people saw it, they fell on their faces: and they said, Yahveh, He is God; Yahveh, He is God. And Elijah said to them, Take the prophets of Baal; don't let one of them escape. *They took them, and Elijah brought them down to the brook Kishon, and killed them there. Elijah said to Ahab, Get you up, eat and drink, for there is the sound of abundance of rain.*
—*1 Kings* 18:31-41

Only after the judgment fire from Heaven fell on the sacrifice of Elijah did the people repent, and only after Elijah had slaughtered the false priests and prophets, he released the rain. In the same way Yeshua is judging His house worldwide in these End Times in order to bring forth revival and the great harvest. Are you ready?

Judgment must first begin in the House of Yah before revival can come, and the first ones to be judged are the priests and the prophets; those who have been prophesying falsely, the soothsayers that caress the ears of the flock and those that lead the people astray with false teaching that does not produce righteousness, holiness and devotion to the Most High!

The holy angels are ready to bring the winds of revival and the End Time harvest, in order to fulfill Yah's words spoken by His prophets of old and His modern-day prophets, in order to answer the prayers of the many saints and holy intercessors. But is His house ready? Is the church ready?

> "For the time [has come] for judgment to begin at the house of God. If it begins first at us, what will happen to those who don't obey the gospel of God?"
> —1 Peter 4:17

CHAPTER SEVEN
The Dynamics of Judgment

"For the time [has come] for judgment to begin at the house of God. If it begins first at us, what will happen to those who don't obey the gospel of God?"
—1 Peter 4:17

These extreme weather patterns and especially their connection with the way that nations behave toward Israel and/or their internal moral condition should warn us that there is surely more to come. Such was the case with Sodom and Gomorrah in ancient times. They were destroyed by fire and brimstone because of their rampant homosexuality and sodomy (which bears a remarkable resemblance to the fresh devastation in New Orleans – the seat of shameless homosexuality - by hurricane Katrina).

However, we need to understand that the Creator is just and He will first judge His own before He judges the whole earth. The same happened with Israel 2000 years ago when they missed the time of their visitation by the first coming of Messiah, and so we were exiled for almost 2000 years before He restored us back to His Land. He has judged Israel for 2000 years, now He will judge the church, and lastly, He will judge all the earth. These hurricanes and tsunamis are already the beginning of His judgment - Let him that has an ear, hear what the spirit is saying to the churches! Judgment and revival are knocking on the doors of the church worldwide.

What Are the Main Purposes of the Judgment of God?

> "You pronounced judgment from heaven. The earth feared, and was silent, When God arose to judgment, to save all the afflicted ones of the earth. Selah."
> —Psalm 76:8-9

1. To restore the fear of Yahveh on the earth
2. To save the afflicted ones, the humble ones that cannot save themselves and set them free from the wicked that oppress them.

> "With my soul have I desired you in the night; yes, with my spirit within me will I seek you earnestly: for when your judgments are in the earth, the inhabitants of the world learn righteousness."
> —Isaiah 26:9

Judgments of Yah open our hearts to learn His righteous ways and commandments because the fear of Yah (God) is restored into our lives.

> "[seek him] who makes the Pleiades and Orion, and turns the shadow of death into the morning, and makes the day dark with night; who calls for the wa-

ters of the sea, and pours them out on the surface of the earth (Yahveh is His name); who brings sudden destruction on the strong, so that destruction comes on the fortress."

—Amos 5:8,9

3. His judgments cause people to seek **Him**

"So pursue them with your tempest, terrify them with your storm. Fill their faces with confusion, that they may seek your name, Yahveh. Let them be put to shame and dismayed forever. Yes, let them be confounded and perish; that they may know that you alone, whose name is Yahveh, Are the Most High over all the earth."

—Psalm 83:15-18

4. So that the rebellious will seek His name and stop calling on other gods!

5. That the wicked may know His name Yahveh and that He is the Most High God!

The reason why Yah's judgment must begin in His house and among His people is so that they may be prepared to stand when He judges others. We are called to be a Royal Priesthood but we must sanctify ourselves to be ready to officiate during Stormy Weather. We must be ready to stand in the gap, pray, intercede, preach, exhort and rescue those of the earth who are meek and needy and trapped in the midst of Yah's judgment. We are His rescue team, His conquering

Joshua's, His Mercy poured out; but we need to be holy and righteous so that we may not be a casualty or a stumbling block but rather a lighthouse, to rescue and direct people in the midst of the storms. We are called to officiate a mighty outpouring of holiness and righteousness, a mighty revival with signs, wonders and miracles and great fruit following - right in the eye of the storm - but we need to be sanctified *first*!

Before the conquest of the Promised Land there were two things that Joshua commanded the people to do:

1. To sanctify themselves before the miracle of crossing the Jordan River on dry land. "Joshua said to the people, sanctify yourselves; for tomorrow Yahveh will do wonders among you." (Joshua 3:5)
1. To get circumcised prior to possessing the Promised Land.

"At that time Yahveh said to Joshua, Make you flint knives, and circumcise again the children of Israel the second t i m e .

Joshua made himself flint knives, and circumcised the children of Israel at the hill of the foreskins. This is why Joshua did circumcise: all the people who came forth out of Egypt, who were males, even all the men of war, died in the wilderness by the way, after they came forth out of Egypt. For all the people who came out were circumcised; but all the people who were born in the wilderness by the way as they came forth out of Egypt, they had not circumcised. For the children of Israel walked forty years in the wilderness, until all the nation, even the men of war who came forth out of Egypt, were consumed, because they didn't listen to the voice of Yahveh: to whom Yahveh swore that he wouldn't let them see the land which Yahveh swore to their fathers that he would give us, a land flowing with milk and honey. Their children, whom he raised up in their place, them did Joshua circumcise: for they were uncircumcised, because they had not circumcised them by the way. It happened, when they had done circumcising all the nation, that they abode in their places in the camp, until they were whole. Yahveh said to Joshua, This day have I rolled away the reproach of Egypt from off you. Therefore the name of that place was called Gilgal, to this day. The children of Israel encamped in Gilgal, and they kept the Passover on the fourteenth day of the month at even in the plains of Jericho. They ate of the produce of the land on the next day after the Passover, unleavened cakes and parched grain, in the same day. The manna ceased on the next day, after they had eaten of the produce of the land; neither had the children of Israel manna anymore; but they ate of the fruit of the land of Canaan that year."

—Joshua 5:2-12

Please read this passage carefully in order to understand what the spirit is saying to His people!

1. The people of Israel had to be circumcised for the second time.
2. They had not been circumcised on the way, though they enjoyed the presence of His glory in the form of a cloud and a pillar of fire.
3. The past generation that sinned against Yah did not get to enter into the promises!
4. The new generation was going to possess the Promised Land only after they were circumcised.
5. This circumcision rolled away the reproach of Egypt and removed any shame left from the bondage and slavery of the past. So, this painful process was going to bring great healing.
6. Immediately after the circumcision, they celebrated Passover, the Feast that represents them being spared the judgment of Egypt through the death of the first born. In the same way, a circumcised (of heart) church will be spared the wrath of God.
7. Immediately after the circumcision and the celebration of Passover, they began to inherit the promises and began to eat the fruit of the land!

The ceremony of circumcision is the token of the Covenant made between Elohim and Abraham. Later on, this token would be fulfilled in the Gentiles also, as they would receive the circumcision of the heart when they repented of their sins and accepted Messiah Yeshua. The sign that a heart is circumcised is that it has the Commandments of God written in it; thus a person with a circumcised heart is no longer rebellious against the Most High and His ways but rather seeks to please Him and glorify His Name in all things!

The foreskin (superfluous flesh) of his heart would have been removed and a tender heart would become sensitive to Yah's Commandments and to His voice. Humility and obedience are the fruits of a circumcised heart.

It is very enlightening to note that Elijah the Prophet went to Gilgal (the place of the circumcision) prior to being taken to heaven in a whirlwind. So it is with this Elijah generation that is preparing the return of the King.

> "And it came to pass, when Jehovah would take up Elijah by a whirlwind into heaven, that Elijah went with Elisha from Gilgal."
>
> —2 Kings 2:1

We are also being prepared to be taken up in a whirlwind in a day soon to come; first in a whirlwind of revival in the midst of judgment and then when the heavenly shofar blows:

> "For the Lord himself shall descend from heaven, with a shout, with the voice of the archangel, and with the trump of God: and the dead in Christ shall rise first; then we that are alive, that are left, shall together with them be caught up in the clouds, to

meet the Lord in the air: and so shall we ever be with the Lord."

—1 Thessalonians 4:16-17

But for that to happen we have to be circumcised a second time and remove the reproach of Babylon and replacement theology that has kept the church in bondage for over 1600 years! (See appendix 2 and 3 at the end of the book) Then, we will enjoy a whirlwind of revival - and then the whirlwind up to Heaven just like Elijah!

"Circumcise therefore the foreskin of your heart, and be no more stiff-necked."

—Deuteronomy 10:16

"Yahveh your God will circumcise your heart, and the heart of your seed, to love Yahveh your God with all your heart, and with all your soul, that you may live."

—Deuteronomy 30:6

"For he is not a Jew who is one outwardly, neither is that circumcision which is outward in the flesh; but he is a Jew who is one inwardly, and circumcision is that of the heart, in the spirit not in the letter; whose praise is not from men, but from God."

—Romans 2:28,29

> "For we are the circumcision, who worship God in the spirit, and rejoice in Messiah Yeshua, and have no confidence in the flesh"
>
> —Philippians 3:3

Yahveh had His people Israel circumcised prior to them possessing the Promised Land so that they would not do it by might, nor by power, but by His spirit; so they wouldn't boast that their might got them all that prosperity, but rather the hand of Yah fulfilling His Covenant with Abraham.

For us to be Priests and Kings of the coming revival we need to get sanctified and get circumcised of heart.

If we are to stand in the gap and rescue a dying world we need to repent first and then take our stand for revival!

At this present time the rate of immorality in the church (most any church) is extremely high and especially among pastors and leaders. There is a breakdown in leadership and in the family, with the rate of divorce matching and even surpassing that of the 'world'. There are spiritual winds and storms passing through many churches which are 'blowing many people away' from the church. There is an entire young generation that will not set foot in any church building. There are countless hungry and thirsty people who cannot find wholesome food and pure water anywhere. There are many flocks with broken hearts because of the many pastors that have fallen into adultery, and so on …

In order to understand the connection between weather patterns and the judgment of the Most High God, we need to establish the fact that all weather is created by God Himself, in order to *fulfill the word, and most particularly the stormy wind.* Throughout the Holy Scriptures we can see that the Almighty uses winds to fulfill His word and will. (Even those that men are planning to manipulate like in the HAARP project. Notice that the magicians of Pharaoh in Egypt could imitate the signs that Moses did, until the point where Moses' snake ate all the others. The true authority and signs of Yahveh are always greater and swallow all the other ones! Exodus 7:10-13)

> "Praise Yahveh from the earth, you great sea creatures, and all depths! Lightning and hail, snow and clouds; Stormy wind, fulfilling His word;"
>
> —*Psalm* 148:7,8

Yeshua warned His disciples about the coming winds and storms. His Word warns us to this day that the only way to withstand the winds and the storms (that would surely come) is to be established on a *solid foundation of His Word.* Unfortunately for the most part, the church as a whole is on a very shaky foundation because it has rejected most of God's law as irrelevant for today and with that it has discarded the most valuable - the very foundational part of the Holy Scriptures - namely the five Books of Moses or the Book of the Law, and it has wrongly misinterpreted most all of the other books including the New Testament! Since the Council of Nicaea in 325 AD, the Torah, or the Book of The Law, has been discarded by most of Christianity, thus the church as a whole is not ready to withstand the storms that are still to come prior to the return of Messiah!

"The rain came down, the floods came, and the winds blew, and beat on that house, and it didn't fall, for it was founded on the rock. Everyone who hears these words of mine, and doesn't do them will be like a foolish man, who built his house on the sand. The rain came down, the floods came, and the winds blew, and beat on that house, and it fell -- and great was its fall."

—Matthew 7:25-27

"Don't think that I came to destroy the law or the prophets. I didn't come to destroy, but to fulfill. For most assuredly, I tell you, until heaven and earth pass away, not even one smallest letter or one tiny pen stroke shall in any way pass away from the law, until all things are accomplished. Whoever, therefore, shall break one of these least commandments, and teach others to do so, shall be called least in the Kingdom of Heaven, but whoever shall do and teach them shall be called great in the Kingdom of Heaven.
For I tell you, that unless your righteousness exceeds that of the scribes and Pharisees, there is no way you shall enter into the Kingdom of Heaven."

—Matthew 5:17-20

The master warned us that not everyone will come in:

> "Not everyone who says to me, 'Lord, Lord, will enter into the Kingdom of Heaven, but he who does the will of my father who is in heaven. Many will tell me in that day, 'Lord, Lord, didn't we prophesy by your name, by your name cast out demons, and by your name do many mighty works? 'Then I will tell them, 'I never knew you. Depart from me, you who work iniquity."
>
> —Matthew 7:21-23

The word iniquity here in Greek signifies 'lawlessness' or 'without law'. Countless Christians have been deceived to believe that God's law is done away with and they will be very unpleasantly surprised when they meet Him. How many will be able to escape His coming judgment? And how many pastors and leaders are teaching their flocks to disobey God's Commandments by their own example of immorality and laxity and a false gospel of supposed grace without law?

These are times of great shaking. Just like the winds and the storms are shaking the nations and warning them of the impending judgment, so is the Holy Spirit, as a mighty rushing wind and a strong shofar blow, warning us that we must repent and return to the original Jewish foundations of the gospel that the ancient Jewish apostles and disciples in Jerusalem had. It is truly time to go back to the Book of the Acts of the Apostles! Not only to the miracles, but also to the obedience to the voice (spirit) and the word (Law- Torah) of the Almighty; to the fear of Yahveh that was upon them all and upon all those who heard their message and even came close to them!

> "Thus says Yahveh, stand you in the ways and see, and ask for the old paths, where is the good way; and walk therein, and you shall find rest for your souls: but they said, we will not walk [therein]. I set watchmen over you, [saying], listen to the sound of the trumpet; but they said, we will not listen. Therefore hear, you nations, and know, congregation, what is among them. Hear, earth: behold, I will bring evil on these people, even the fruit of their thoughts, because they have not listened to my words; and as for my law, they have rejected it."
> —Jeremiah 6:16-19

The church has been either bored to death through a lifeless and powerless religion or entertained to death by the supposed livelier charismatic groups. Both of them are bringing death instead of life, one by rejecting the Holy Spirit and the other one by rejecting the Torah, the eternal laws of the Creator, that the spirit of truth has been sent to teach us!

The church is called to set an example as Daniel, who refused to eat unclean animals under threat of death!

> "But Daniel purposed in his heart that he would not defile himself with the king's dainties, nor with the wine which he drank: therefore he requested of

the prince of the eunuchs that he might not defile himself. Now God made Daniel to find kindness and compassion in the sight of the prince of the eunuchs. The prince of the eunuchs said to Daniel, I fear my lord the king, who has appointed your food and your drink: for why should he see your faces worse looking than the youths who are of your own age? So would you endanger my head with the king? Then said Daniel to the steward whom the prince of the eunuchs had appointed over Daniel, Hananiah, Mishael, and Azariah: Prove your servants, I beg you, ten days; and let them give us pulse to eat, and water to drink. Then let our faces be looked on before you, and the face of the youths who eat of the king's dainties; and as you see, deal with your servants. So he listened to them in this matter, and proved them ten days. At the end of ten days their faces appeared fairer, and they were fatter in flesh, than all the youths who ate of the king's dainties."

—Daniel 1:8-15

Many ministries are advocating the idea of going back to the Book of Acts of the Apostles and to the same glory and miracles, however, they totally forget that the first church in Jerusalem and the apostles were Jewish. They knew about the fear of God. You could not convince them to break Shabbat or eat unclean animals or take lying and adultery lightly. They knew the Torah, the laws of the creator, and they had no New Testament book available but only the Hebrew Holy Scriptures. It was in this atmosphere of holy fear of Yahveh and total obedience to Yah's voice (spirit) and Commandments (word) that the awesome and glorious miracles happened. The church world-wide is now challenged by the Almighty to return to the same obedience and to the same holiness. It is time the church repents seriously for rejecting God's Commandments and for taking them lightly in the name of 'spiritual freedom and liberty', the Holy Spirit is none other than the spirit of holiness and He has been sent not only to give us 'goose bumps' but to convict us of sin and lead us into all truth. The spirit of God will never lead you to break His Commandments, but rather enable you to *keep them*.

The Josiah Generation of Holiness and Revival

We are in the same condition that Israel was when King Josiah began to reign and his scribe Shaphan found the Book of the Torah (Law of God) buried under the debris of the temple. When this young king read the Holy Book, he tore his garments as a sign of mourning for breaking the Holy Commandments of a holy God. He immediately sought prophetic advice from the hand of a holy woman, a prophetess by the name of Hulda, who told him that the judgment of God was coming. However, she promised that during the lifetime of King Josiah there would be peace and blessing because the king had repented before Yahveh, the Most High. So, also today Yah is calling this new generation of kings and priests to find the Book of the Law and to tear their garments in mourning for the sins and ignorance of the past generations.

It may be that the Most High will listen to this young new generation and a great revival will break out in their time, maybe the last great revival prior to the outpouring of God's wrath on the earth.

> "Shaphan the scribe told the king, saying, Hilkiah the priest has delivered me a book. Shaphan read it before the king. It happened when the king had heard the words of the Book of the Law, that he tore his clothes. The king commanded Hilkiah the priest, and Ahikam the son of Shaphan, and Achbor the son of Micaiah, and Shaphan the scribe, and Asaiah the king's servant, saying, Go you, inquire of Yahveh for me, and for the people, and for all Judah, concerning the words of this book that is found; for great is the wrath of Yahveh that is kindled against us, because our fathers have not listened to the words of this book, to do according to all that which is written concerning us. So Hilkiah the priest, and Ahikam, and Achbor, and Shaphan, and Asaiah, went to Huldah the prophetess, the wife of Shallum the son of Tikvah, the son of Harhas, keeper of the wardrobe (now she lived in Jerusalem in the second quarter); and they talked with her. She said to them, thus says Yahveh, the God of Israel: Tell you the man who sent

you to me, thus says Yahveh, Behold, I will bring evil on this place, and on the inhabitants of it, even all the words of the book which the king of Judah has read. Because they have forsaken me, and have burned incense to other gods, that they might provoke me to anger with all the work of their hands, therefore my wrath shall be kindled against this place, and it shall not be quenched. But to the king of Judah, who sent you to inquire of Yahveh, thus shall you tell him, thus says Yahveh, the God of Israel: As touching the words which you have heard, because your heart was tender, and you did humble yourself before Yahveh when you heard what I spoke against this place, and against the inhabitants of it, that they should become a desolation and a curse, and have torn your clothes, and wept before me; I also have heard you, says Yahveh. Therefore, behold, I will gather you to your fathers, and you shall be gathered to your grave in peace, neither shall your eyes see all the evil which I will bring on this place. They brought the king word again"

—2 Kings 22:10-22

2,000 years ago Yaacov (James) the brother of Yeshua the Messiah addressed a serious situation among the believers of His day, and His prescription was the same as the one in this chapter. We need to repent for breaking God's Commandments and for forsaking His ways!

Where do wars and fighting among you come from? Don't they come from your pleasures that war in your members? You lust, and don't have. You kill, covet, and can't obtain. You fight and make war. Yet you don't have, because you don't ask. You ask and don't receive, because you ask amiss, so that you may spend it for your pleasures. You adulterers and adulteresses, don't you know that friendship with the world is enmity with God? Whoever therefore wants to be a friend of the world makes himself an enemy of God. Or do you think that the Scripture says in vain, "The spirit who lives in us yearns jealously"? But He gives more grace. Therefore it says, "God resists the proud, but gives grace to the humble." Be subject therefore to God. But resist the devil, and he will flee from you. *Draw near to God, and He will draw near to you. Cleanse your hands, you sinners; and purify your hearts, you double-minded. Lament, mourn, and weep.* Let your laughter be turned to mourning, and your joy to gloom. Humble yourselves in the sight of the Lord, and He will exalt you. Don't speak against one another, brothers. He who speaks against a brother and judges his brother, speaks against the law and judges the law. But if you judge the law, you are not a doer of the law, but a judge. Only one is the lawgiver, who is able to save and to destroy. But who are you to judge another? Come now, you who say,

"Today or tomorrow let's go into this city, and spend a year there, and trade, and get gain." Whereas you don't know what your life will be like tomorrow. For what is your life? For you are a vapor, that appears for a little time, and then vanishes away. For you ought to say, "If the Lord wills, we will both live, and do this or that." But now you glory in your boasting. All such boasting is evil. To him therefore who knows to do good, and doesn't do it, to him it is sin"

—Yaacov (James) 4

An Important Prayer

If you already feel convicted that you are not walking in holiness and righteousness, though you may be a Christian or a Jew, it is the father's grace that is drawing you to Him so you might repent and return to Him and to His holy standards and ways.

Pray with Me

Dear Father in heaven, thank you so much for giving me the gift of repentance. I am terribly sorry for breaking your commandments and forsaking your ways through my own ignorance, rebelliousness and selfishness. I truly repent from the bottom of my heart and renounce my old ungodly ways. Please write your laws and Commandments in my heart that I may serve you in spirit and truth. I thank you for this second chance to be restored to You and to Your Kingdom. Here I am Lord, change me and use me for the glory of your holy name. I forsake all other masters, people, sins that have had a grip on me and I worship/serve/obey You alone. In Yeshua's name. Amen.

CHAPTER EIGHT

Repentance & Restitution

The Key of Abraham

There was a famine in the days of David three years, year after year; and David sought the face of Yahveh. Yahveh said, it is for Saul, and for his bloody house, because he put to death the Gibeonites. The king called the Gibeonites and said to them (now the Gibeonites were not of the children of Israel, but of the remnant of the Amorites; and the children of Israel had sworn to them: and Saul sought to kill them in his zeal for the children of Israel and Judah.)
—2 Samuel 21:1,2

There is a time when Yah's people suffer for the sins of past generations as in the case of King David. He was not to blame for the sins of Saul but nevertheless he reaped the consequences. In this case it was drought and famine. We can clearly see that his response was not to shake the responsibility off his shoulders and say, "It's not my fault, I'm OK, it was King Saul's fault". No, in royal style, he took the challenge and repented on behalf of these past sins of his predecessor, not only verbally repenting but also making active restitution.

This is a serious shortcoming and sore point in the church today which is actually withholding a true outpouring of God's grace - repentance from past sins. Active restitution will be the trigger point for the release of His grace throughout the world. The church has much to repent of in the area of past sins towards many peoples, such as the native Americans and South Americans for stealing their land, breaking many treaties and doing hideous things to them in the name of God!

More than anything, it needs to seriously repent for the past sins towards the Jewish people. The hands of the church are stained with the blood of millions of Jews. Church history is for the most part a bloody history. Since the Council of Nicaea (see appendix 3), Christianity has targeted the Jewish people for humiliation, plunder and destruction.

> And David said to the Gibeonites, What shall I do for you? And with what shall I make atonement that you may bless the inheritance of Yahveh?
> —2 Samuel 21:3

The following is an excerpt from the book "The Seasons of The Lord" by Rev. and Prophet William Moreford, the writer of the "Power New Testament":

> The reason Jewish roots were lost early in church history is that our revered church fathers were antisemitic, deliberately changing Jewish celebrations and altering some doctrines to make a complete break

from Judaism. In the second century, Justin martyr, Polycarp, and Marcion were among those beginning the onslaught against the Jewish people and Judaism. Marcion, in the middle of the second century, was the first to write that the New Covenant had replaced all previous covenants - and he was known as a heretic. His writing was later taken seriously and led to replacement theology, the elements of which show up in the Thompson Chain-Reference Bible. On the back of the New Testament title page there is a chart listing contrasts between the Old and New Testaments, including spiritual darkness vs. light of world, death reigns vs. life eternal and fifteen other such comparisons. Jesus and His disciples would not have agreed with that chart. Jesus said, "Do not think that I came to abolish the Torah... (Matthew 5:17-20)

In the fourth century, John Chrysostom, known for powerful, eloquent sermons, gave a series of seventeen virulently anti- Semitic sermons at a time when the pagan celebration of Ishtar (Easter), the fertility goddess, was set to replace Passover as the celebration of Jesus' death and resurrection. Also, the Roman winter solstice celebration, in honor of the god Saturn, was established as the celebration of Jesus' birth. In the fifth century, Augustine brought

Greek philosophy into Christian theology, which has influenced the church to this day.

The celebrations introduced in the fourth century put a seal on the separation from Judaism and set the stage for violence against the Jewish people. Jewish people even today often view Christians as "the enemy" with good reason. Over the centuries Christians have outperformed all other groups combined in the killing of Jews. There were numerous pogroms throughout Europe from early on through to the Holocaust. In medieval Spain, children at the age of eight, were taken from Jewish parents to be raised in Christian homes. Jews were frequently forced to convert to Christianity, then afterward were still persecuted for being Jewish. In 1492 Ferdinand and Isabella forced the Jews to leave Spain. Such forced exoduses were common, with Jews moving from one country to another, virtually all over Europe. Every European country has expelled Jews at least once. Jews were forbidden to own land until they came to the American colonies. The Spanish Inquisition is well known for cruelty to the Jews.

The Holocaust was not the end of antisemitism and not the sole evidence of it during WW II. During the Holocaust, not one Christian denomination spoke out against the attempted extermination of the Jewish people. The US government turned away a ship loaded with Jewish refugees from Europe and forced it to return, which meant certain death for the passengers. US bombers flew over Auschwitz nearly every night to bomb railroad marshalling yards just a few miles away, but never bombed the gas chambers, seemingly to "avoid possible collateral damage, killing or injuring prisoners" who were going to be gassed in the very near future. Today, antisemitism is rising throughout the world, especially in Europe. It is very strong in the UN.

To understand the Jewish roots of Christianity, look first to the Hebrew Scriptures. Among the first things the early church did to divorce itself from Judaism was to change the seasons of the Lord. These are detailed in Leviticus 23, beginning with the Sabbath. The church at Constantine's, behest moved Jesus' death and resurrection from Passover to Easter, then added Christmas to celebrate Jesus' birth. His birth, death, and resurrection certainly need to be honored, but not with pagan holidays.

As the church returns to its Jewish Roots it is not to copy modern Judaism, to be pretend Jews. The church needs to study Scripture, honoring the commandments that have been forsaken, becoming worshipers in spirit and in truth."

Love and blessings, Rev. Bill Moreford (from his book *The Seasons of the Lord*)

The reason why entire nations are closed to revival is because there is too much Jewish blood in their ground and on their hands. Such is the case for most of Europe. Hatred of Jews is the number one cause for the withholding of revival and for the release of judgment as we have seen in chapters one to three of this book. The church is now being judged for the sins of past generations, and her response to this judgment will either release or withhold revival or release or withhold judgment in entire regions and entire nations. This is the key of Abraham for End Time revival or judgment 16. There is a "David generation" that is called to rise to this task.

> "I will bless those who bless you, and I will curse him who curses you. In you will all of the families of the earth be blessed."
>
> —Genesis 12:3

King David's response determined the fate of Israel, whether drought, famine, death or rain and blessing..

> And David said to the Gibeonites, What shall I do for you? And with what shall I make atonement that you may bless the inheritance of Yahveh?
>
> —2 Samuel 21:3

This should be the question of every Christian and every Christian church, every denomination and stream of Christianity representing every nation in the face of the earth: "And David said to the Gibeonites, What shall I do for you? And with what shall I make atonement that you may bless the inheritance of Yahveh?"

Only when churches and the church worldwide (every part of it) rises up to repent and bless Israel actively, both in prayers and speech and monetarily; then will Yah hear the pleading of His saints in their nations. That is the reason why so many prayers for harvest and revival go unanswered because restitution towards His Jewish people has never been made. Revival can start with you, your church and your denominations if you respond to this message. Judgment has already begun in the house of Yahveh so* I suggest that you read my book "Sheep Nations" on this most important subject.

"Let him that has an ear hear what the ruach is saying to the churches!"

Revival can begin with you and your congregation repenting for the sins of past generations and making active restitution. True acts of restitution will trigger a response from the Jewish people, as they will arise to bless the church. Many times when we are sent to the nations, I pray and hope that people will get the revelation of repentance and restitution towards us, so we can bless them. Anywhere where we are received as Jewish apostles sent from Jerusalem and blessed, I make it a point to release people

---

* Order from www.kad-esh.org or info@kad-esh.org

from their bondages and curses and to release revival winds and holy fire. Many amazing miracles and healings have occurred in our ministry because of that. The blessing of a Jew carries great weight in the spirit to a church that owes us a tremendous amount of restitution, and the Almighty confirms His Word with signs and wonders and miracles.

However, the same is true if we're not received, but are rejected and financial and personal blessings are withheld. In that case judgment can follow. Yah is very touchy about this issue as the history of the church with the Jews is so bloody and so tragic that it demands a heavenly response of total judgment. I am writing this book because I have stood in the gap for the church for sixteen years and have suffered a lot at the hands of misguided Christian leaders and people who have harmed us because of the message that we carry. I have wept many tears in intercession for those foolish and prideful, ignorant leaders who have rejected our message and have closed entire areas, nations and continents for revival. I truly pray that you, my reader, would understand the seriousness of this message and would respond accordingly. It is in your hands to bring revival, blessing or judgment upon your life, your family, your church or your nation concerning this issue. One way that you can make active restitution is to help us through your prayers and finances to bring this message to the ends of the earth, so the drought can break and revival can come. You can also train with us and join us as we are recruiting End Time soldiers. There is a great harvest that will be lost if we do not do this *quickly*! (Please see information on the back page or communicate with us through www.kad-esh.org).

> The harvest is past, the summer is ended, and we are not saved. For the hurt of the daughter of my people am I hurt: I mourn; dismay hath taken hold on me. Is there no balm in Gilead? Is there no physician there? Why then is not the health of the daughter of my people recovered?
>
> —Jeremiah 8:20-22

I was leading a tour through the death camps of Poland a few years ago. As I walked through the forests of Sobibor, where there are numerous unmarked Jewish graves and many ashes from the crematoriums that used to be there, I heard terrible cries. The place was totally silent; there was no one but us there. The cries of men, women and children, and even babies, terrible tormented cries intensified in my ears. I asked the others if they were hearing anything and they all had the same experience and gave me the same report. The blood of our Jewish brethren was crying from the ground. And so it is in many nations.

> Yahveh said to Cain, "Where is Abel, your brother?" He said, "I don't know. Am I my brother's keeper?" Yahveh said, "What have you done? The voice of your brother's blood cries to me from the ground. Now you are cursed because of the ground, which

has opened its mouth to receive your brother's blood from your hand. From now on, when you till the ground, it won't yield its strength to you. You shall be a fugitive and a wanderer in the earth."

—Genesis 4:9-12

The church needs to come home to Israel, to the original apostolic Jewish foundations: She has been a wanderer, in exile for too long.

Please make a pause here. Consider this chapter seriously.

A Prayer of Repentance for Past Sins

Dear father in heaven, I realize that I, and my predecessors in the church, have sinned against Your people Israel. Our hands are stained with Jewish blood. I ask Your forgiveness and cry out for Your mercy dear heavenly father. I also ask You for forgiveness for the vast majority of the church who are in deception and are permitting the land of Israel to be divided and stolen in order to establish a Palestinian terror state. Father, please have mercy over Your church and wake us up, that we may arise and make restitution for the sins of all our ancestors since the infamous Council of Nicaea until now. We have sinned greatly and we need all Your mercy. Please bring forth true repentance for this sin worldwide. In Yeshua's name, amen.

For more on the subject please read my books "The Healing Power of the Roots", "Sheep Nations" and "Grafted In" so you may be discipled in the holy ways of the Almighty. Also connect with us and tell us that you have prayed this prayer so we can pray for you and help you by visiting www.kad-esh.org or emailing info@kad-esh.org

CHAPTER NINE
Coming to the Original Foundations

"If the foundations are being destroyed what can the righteous do?"
—Psalm 11:3

During stormy weather what is most tested is the foundation of a house or a building. If the foundations are solid, then the house will be able to stay standing through the storm with minor or no damage. We may have the most beautiful furniture, the most exquisite jewels, door handles made out of gold, china in the bathrooms and state of the art stained glass windows but all those will be of no help during storms or earthquakes; it is only the foundation of that house that will determine if the house will stand or not.

The church of the twenty-first century, especially in the West, has all the dressings and the trappings. In some cases it is like a well-oiled machine with everything necessary to present an attractive gospel to the masses, including smoke machines on the altar and flashing lights but what about the foundations? Are they strong enough, true enough to withstand rough weather (spiritually or physically)? I do not think so. I have met too many believers who get angry with God and go into sin in order to compensate themselves for the hardships they are going through. The standards of holiness and righteousness in the people and even in the leadership are so low, that any little shaking causes them to be uprooted from the truth. If there is a problem in the church world-wide it is a foundational problem.

First let us take a look at the foundations of the New Jerusalem:

> "One of the seven angels who had the seven bowls, who were laden with the seven last plagues came, and He spoke with me, saying, "Come here. I will show you the wife, the lamb's bride." He carried me away in the spirit to a great and high mountain, and showed me the holy city, Jerusalem, coming down out of heaven from God, having the glory of God. Her light was like a most precious stone, as if it was a jasper stone, clear as crystal; having a great and high wall; having twelve gates, and at the gates twelve angels; and names written on them, which are the names of the twelve tribes of the children of Israel. On the east were three gates, and on the north three gates, and on the south three gates, and on the west three gates. The wall of the city had twelve foundations, and on them twelve names of the twelve apostles of the lamb.
>
> —Revelation 21:9-14

Let us take a closer look at the New Jerusalem, the wife of the lamb; this is who we are!

The first thing that we see about her is that she is shining with the glory of God and the second thing that we see is her structure, the manner in which she is built. So there must be a connection between this structure and the glory!

In Hebrew the word "glory" is *kavod*. It means weighty, heavy, prosperous, awesomely beautiful, luxurious and honorable with heavy authority, someone to reckon with.

This city, the New Jerusalem - the wife of the lamb is all of those things! And we are prepared to be just like this description in Revelation 21, but for us to achieve this purpose we need to pay careful attention to her structure:

> Having a great and high wall; having twelve gates, and at the gates twelve angels; and names written on them, which are the names of the twelve tribes of the children of Israel.

1. We see a great and high wall - symbolizing separation or kdushá in Hebrew, which means holiness! In other words she is separated from other structures and not just anyone can come in. In another Scripture in the same chapter, it says, "There will in no way enter into it anything profane, or one who causes an abomination or a lie, but only those who are written in the lamb's book of life." Revelation 21:27; and yet in another previous verse it says: "But for the cowardly, unbelieving, sinners, abominable, murderers,

sexually immoral, sorcerers, idolaters, and all liars, their part is in the lake that burns with fire and sulfur, which is the second death." (Revelation 21:8)

2. Then we see twelve gates that are named for the twelve tribes of Israel. We do not see any denominational name on it; the names of all the different Christian organizations or denominations of the church of today are not on the gate of entrance but rather the twelve tribes of Israel! So it does not matter if you are a Baptist, a Presbyterian, a Catholic, a Charismatic, or Prophetic, an Apostolic or a non-denominational - your only way to come in is through "The Pearly Gates" and they bear the name of Israel! In Romans 11, the Apostle Shaul- Paul said the Gentiles are grafted into the olive tree - which is Israel through faith in the Jewish Messiah. Paul also says the Gentiles are nourished from the rich root of the olive tree; that they should be careful to maintain themselves in humility concerning the natural branches - the Jews - because the Gentiles do not support the root, but the root supports the Gentiles. Therefore a right attitude of humility from the Gentles to Israel is needed in order to be part of this New Jerusalem. The Gentiles are not grafted into the tree of knowledge, nor the Christmas tree but into the olive tree, which is Israel. Let us remember: A right relationship is needed between the Gentiles and Israel. (Romans 11:11-24) "But if some of the branches were broken off, and you, being a wild olive, were grafted in among them, and became partaker with them of the root of

the richness of the olive tree; don't boast over the branches. But if you boast, it is not you who bear the root, but the root you." (Romans 11:27-28)

The wall of the city had twelve foundations, and on them twelve names of the twelve apostles of the lamb.

3. Thirdly we see the foundations of the city. Here again we do not see any great names from past revivals, not even of great Christian reformers but rather the names of the twelve apostles of the lamb. In other words the foundations of the city, by which this glorious New Jerusalem stands, are twelve Jewish men that were chosen by the Messiah Himself. They are not just any apostles, but rather the apostles of the lamb! Not even Paul, the Apostle to the Gentiles, is mentioned here but rather the twelve original ones. They all knew Yeshua personally! In other words the words that the master said to them are the foundational stones of our faith and of the New Jerusalem. So, the foundations of the New Jerusalem are not the Christian doctrines espoused by St. Augustine, John Chrysostom or even Martin Luther. The foundational doctrines of the church (Hebrew-*Adá*-Congregation of witnesses) were handed to the twelve Jewish Apostles. In order to have a solid foundation we need to return to the original foundations of the church and they are Jewish.

As I mentioned before, the only thing that matters during stormy weather is how well the foundations are built, and secondly how well the structure is built. We can see here that the New Jerusalem is filled with glory (*kavod*) because she is built on the original Jewish foundations and the structure with the twelve gates and the high wall are Israelite.

Now, let me tell you why the church is not ready for the coming revival.

The church at large is not standing on the original Jewish foundations. In fact for the most part the church is hardly recognizable as being grafted into the olive tree - being Israel. Since 1967 Yah has been pouring out His spirit in order to restore His Bride to her Jewish foundations, but many have been so scared of it because of the lies of *replacement theology*[*] that they have shunned it altogether. In my book "The Healing Power of The Roots" I explain that God told me that returning the church back to its original apostolic, Jewish roots foundation was a matter of life and death. Before more stormy weather happens and before revival hits we'd better get back to the original foundations! I wrote three books to help you in this transition, "The Healing Power of the Roots", "Sheep Nations" and "Grafted In". You need the three of them in order to be prepared for the revival to come!

Let me explain something: When revival comes it's like a storm:

> "Now when the day of Pentecost had come, they were all with one accord in one place. Suddenly there came from the sky a sound like the rushing of

---

[*] Read Appendix 2 at the end of this book about replacement theology

a mighty wind, and it filled all the house where they were sitting."

—Acts 2:1-2

When the glory of Yah is revealed it shakes everything,

"In the year that King Uzziah died I saw the Lord sitting on a throne, high and lifted up; and His train filled the temple. Above Him stood the seraphim: each one had six wings; with two he covered His face, and with two he covered His feet, and with two he did fly. One cried to another, and said, Holy, holy, holy, is Yahveh of Hosts: the whole earth is full of His glory. *The foundations of the thresholds shook at the voice of him who cried, and the house was filled with smoke.*"

—Isaiah 6:1-4

If Yah pours out His glory – weighty, heavy: *kabod* – on the church in the condition that we are in, not yet on the right Jewish holy foundations,* the church will be crushed and die! In His mercy, He has not sent revival yet; but He must because His judgments, being in the form of tempests, hurricanes, earthquakes and stormy weather, are already poured out on the earth, so He needs priests and kings to

---

* By Jewish foundations, I mean the Hebrew Holy Scriptures that is mistakenly called "Old Testament". I do not mean The Talmud, the Kabala or the Rabbinical teachings. Please read my book "Grafted In" in order to restore the original Jewish foundations. www.kad-esh.org

officiate - to rescue the lost, to heal the wounded, to train the disciples and to disciple nations... But we need to repent first; a heart circumcision is needed desperately! We need to return to the original Jewish foundations and the Commandments of God that were lost during the Council of Nicaea in 325 AD and we need to restore our relationship with Israel - our olive tree, from which we need to suck our nourishment.

In the next chapter we will see how to do that.

CHAPTER TEN
The Gospel of Obedience

"But in vain do they worship me, teaching as doctrines the commandments of men.' "For you set aside the commandments of God, and hold tightly to the tradition of men - the washing of pitchers and cups, and you do many other such things." He said to them: "Full well do you reject the commandments of God, that you may keep your tradition"
—Mark 7:7-9

In order to restore the original Jewish apostolic foundation that will enable us to be filled with His glory, to stand during stormy weather and to fill the house with the great End Time harvest, we need to discover the secret of the ancient Jewish apostles who walked in such power, authority and holiness.

Their secret is simply this: Child-like faith that led to complete obedience to Yah's Commandments. That obedience in turn gave them all the authority that they needed to exercise their ministry, as they were under authority to Yah's Commandments!

"When He came into Capernaum, a centurion came to Him, asking him, and saying, "Lord, my servant lies in the house paralyzed, grievously tormented."

Jesus said to him, "I will come and heal him." The centurion answered, "Lord, I'm not worthy for you to come under my roof. Just say the word, and my servant will be healed. For I am also a man under authority, having under myself soldiers. I tell this one, 'Go,' and he goes; and to another, 'Come,' and he comes; and to my servant, 'Do this,' and he does it." When Jesus heard it, He marveled, and said to those who followed, "Most assuredly I tell you, I haven't found so great a faith, not even in Israel. I tell you that many will come from the east and the west, and will sit down with Abraham, and Isaac, and Jacob, in the Kingdom of Heaven, but the sons of the kingdom will be thrown out into the outer darkness. There will be weeping and the gnashing of teeth."

—Matthew 8:5-12

This Roman centurion who was so commended and honored by the master, being a Gentile and a Roman soldier, had detected that Yeshua was under authority to someone higher than Himself. Indeed Yeshua walked in complete obedience to His father's commandments! The secret of Yeshua's miraculous power and authority was not that He was the Son of God; rather that He was totally obedient to His father's commandments and voice. This is the secret and the mystery of His power revealed and communicated to His disciples who demonstrated His Kingdom in astounding power and glory- obedience to the father's Commandments!

It does not matter if you call yourself a Christian or a believer or Messianic or a pastor or apostle or a prophet; the main question is: Are you obedient to the father's Commandments or have you been deceived by replacement theology* which teaches that His law is done away with? Since the church at large divorced from the original Jewish foundations, most of the Bible has been misinterpreted through the eyes of replacement theology. This in turn has formed a powerless, lukewarm church that sorely lacks the holy fear of Yah! For us to go back to the awesome glory that the early church had, we have to go back to the fear of God and to the obedience to His Commandments which they also had.

> "Thus says Yahveh, heaven is my throne, and the earth is my footstool: what manner of house will you build to me? And what place shall be my rest? For all these things has my hand made, and [so] all these things came to be, says Yahveh: but to this man will I look, even to him who is poor and of a contrite spirit, and who trembles at my word."
>
> —Isaiah 66:1-2

Yeshua is speaking to the church of today the very same words that He said to the early Jews:

> "But in vain do they worship me, teaching as doctrines the commandments of men.' "For you set

---

*   Replacement theology – See appendix at the end of the book

> aside the commandments of God, and hold tightly to the tradition of men - the washing of pitchers and cups, and you do many other such things." He said to them: *"Full well do you reject the commandments of God, that you may keep your tradition"*
>
> —Mark 7:7-9

The Christian tradition stemming from the deathly replacement theology says that Yah's law is done away with, that it is obsolete, that we are now free and do not need the law. It even goes to say that if we keep the law we will be in bondage and even be under a curse! But hear the fearsome words of Yeshua, the master Himself. May your ears be circumcised to hear, without the lies and the traditions of men indoctrinated by replacement theology, ringing in your ears!

> "Don't think that I came to destroy the law or the prophets. I didn't come to destroy, but to fulfill. For most assuredly, I tell you, until heaven and earth pass away, not even one smallest letter or one tiny pen stroke shall in any way pass away from the law, until all things are accomplished. Whoever, therefore, shall break one of these least commandments, and teach others to do so, shall be called least in the Kingdom of Heaven, but whoever shall do and teach them shall be called great in the Kingdom of Heaven. For I tell you, that unless your righteousness exceeds that

of the scribes and Pharisees, there is no way you shall enter into the Kingdom of Heaven."

—Matthew 5:17-20

The words of Paul have been seriously misinterpreted by replacement theologian's traditions; yes, and even mistranslated in order to support their heresy!

"For it isn't the hearers of the law who are righteous before God, *but the doers of the law will be justified* (for when Gentiles who don't have the law do by nature the things of the law, these, not having the law, are a law to themselves, in that they show the work of the law written in their hearts, their conscience testifying with them, and their thoughts among themselves accusing or else excusing them) in the day when God will judge the secrets of men, according to my gospel, by Jesus Christ.'

—Romans 2:13-16

There are so many Christian traditions that take precedence over the Commandments of God in the church today. Below are a few examples:

Christian Tradition

The exchanging of Sunday for the true Sabbath on the Seventh Day

"On the seventh day God finished His work which He had made; and He rested on the seventh day from all His work which He had made. God blessed the seventh day, and made it holy because He rested in it from all His work which He had created and made."

—Genesis 2:2–3

The Commandment

"Observe the Sabbath day, to keep it holy, as Yahveh your God commanded you. Six days shall you labor, and do all your work; but the seventh day is a Sabbath to Yahveh your God: [in it] you shall not do any work, you, nor your son, nor your daughter, nor your man-servant, nor your maid-servant, nor your ox, nor your donkey, nor any of your cattle, nor your stranger who is within your gates; that your man-servant and your maid-servant may rest as well as you. You shall remember that you were a servant in the land of Egypt, and Yahveh your God brought you out of there by a mighty hand and by an outstretched arm: therefore Yahveh your God commanded you to keep the Sabbath day."

—Deuteronomy 5:12-14

Christian Tradition

Celebrate Christmas and Easter (from the Greek goddess

Ishtar); both of pagan origins and both celebrated at the wrong times! (Christmas and Easter are not mentioned in the Bible as they are of pagan origin - For more about this subject please order my book "Grafted In")

The Commandment

> "Yahveh spoke to Moses, saying, speak to the children of Israel, and tell them, *The set feasts of Yahveh, which you shall proclaim to be holy convocations, even these are my set feasts.* Six days shall work be done: but on the seventh day is a Sabbath of solemn rest, a holy convocation; you shall do no manner of work: it is a Sabbath to Yahveh in all your dwellings. These are the set feasts of Yahveh, even holy convocations, which you shall proclaim in their appointed season. In the first month, on the fourteenth day of the month at even, *is Yahveh's Passover ...*"
> —Leviticus 23:1-5

And then He proceeds to tell us about all of His Holy Feasts and Convocations. Notice that they are the *set feasts of Yahveh and not the tradition of men. Men cannot remove them at will.*

Christian Tradition

Eat whatever is put in front of you. Countless Christians are seriously sick because of this tradition.

> "For every creature of God is good, and nothing is to be rejected, if it is received with thanksgiving. For it is sanctified through *the word of God and prayer.*"
> —1 Timothy 4:4,5.

Christian tradition divorced from the Hebrew Holy Scriptures (mistakenly called Old Testament) has misinterpreted this verse to say that a Christian can and should eat anything. However, this verse talks about the sanctification of the food through two things:

1. *The Word of God* – The only Word at that time, in the first century, was the Hebrew Holy Scriptures. The New Testament was only canonized 300 years later! The Word of Yah does not sanctify any pork, shellfish, snake, blood, fat of animals or any unclean animal. You can pray as much as you want, it is still not sanctified. Yah can protect you from its harmful effects if you eat it in ignorance and without your knowledge but there will be no protection if you eat it to prove your Christian tradition right! That is why countless numbers of Christians are sick. Even after they get miraculously healed they get sick again because they go back to eating the same!
2. *Prayer* – Thanksgiving and protection from all harmful things we are not aware of (like the mad cow disease or SARS for example).

The Commandment

"This is the law of the animal, and of the bird, and of every living creature that moves in the waters, and of every creature that creeps on the earth; to make a distinction between the unclean and the clean, and between the living thing that may be eaten and the living thing that may not be eaten." Leviticus 11 (please read the whole chapter!) "It shall be a perpetual statute throughout your generations in all your dwellings, that you shall eat neither fat nor blood."
—Leviticus 3:17

How many people are deathly ill today because they eat unclean animals or fat or blood?

Christian Tradition in Many Churches

Do not dance or move your body as this is of the devil (especially if women do it!). This tradition is keeping many churches quite dry and powerless.

The Commandment

Praise Yah! Praise God in His sanctuary! Praise Him in His heavens for His acts of power! Praise Him for His mighty acts! Praise Him according to His excellent greatness! Praise Him with the sounding of the trumpet! Praise Him with harp and lyre! *Praise Him with tambourine and dancing!* Praise Him with

> stringed instruments and flute! Praise Him with loud cymbals! Praise Him with resounding cymbals! Let everything that has breath praise Yah! Praise Yah!"
> —Genesis 9:1-6

And that is why the master went so far as to say that in order to inherit eternal life (which also means abundant life on this earth!) we need to keep the Commandments.

> Behold, one came to Him and said, "Good teacher, what good thing shall I do, that I may have eternal life?" He said to him, "Why do you call me good? No one is good but one, that is, God. *But if you want to enter into life, keep the commandments.*" He said to him, "Which ones?" Yeshua said, "You shall not kill. You shall not commit adultery. You shall not steal. You shall not offer false testimony. Honor your father and mother. And, you shall love your neighbor as yourself." The young man said to him, "All these things I have observed from my youth. What do I still lack?" Yeshua said to him, "If you want to be perfect, go, sell what you have, and give to the poor, and you will have treasure in heaven, and come, follow me."
> —Matthew 19:16-20

Notice that Yeshua did not even offer the man a job in His ministry, until he was proven to be one that kept the Commandments. Yeshua invited him to become one of His disciples, maybe even one of His apostles, but he was not chosen for his gifts and talents, or for his money, or for his good looks and connections. No, Yeshua offered him the job because this rich man was obedient to the Commandments!* Of course this rich man did not pass the test that we all need to go through in order to follow the master - to keep the first Commandment, which is:

> "And you shall love Yahveh your God with all your heart, and with all your soul, and with all your might"
> —Deuteronomy 6:5

This rich young man did not keep the Commandments perfectly. He did honor his father and mother, he didn't lie or commit adultery, but he was lacking in obedience to the first commandment:

> "You shall have no other gods before Me"
> —Deuteronomy 5:7

Mammon, money and possessions were the gods of this young man! However, the answer of Yeshua is the same for all of us today,

"But if you want to enter into life, keep the commandments."

---

* In order to learn how to walk in obedience to Yahveh's Commandments in the New Covenant, please read my book and End Time manual of discipleship "Grafted In". Purchase at www.kad-esh.org or info@kad-esh.org

Yeshua came to restore us to obedience to His father. His gospel is not only a gospel of salvation; it is a gospel of obedience.

The great commission that He gave to His Jewish apostles and early disciples was to make disciples and to teach them to observe His Commandments. This great commission has not been answered yet because replacement theology has undermined the great commission since the fourth century and the signing of the Council of Nicaea.[*] Another gospel has been preached and even in the twenty-first Century, at this late hour when the stormy weather of Yah's judgments is blowing all over the nations, the true gospel of obedience is not yet preached. I hope that you, my reader will answer the high call to obedience and to preach this lost, forgotten and true gospel!

> "Go, and make disciples of all nations, baptizing them...*teaching them to observe all things which I commanded you.* Behold, I am with you always, even to the end of the age." Amen.
>
> —Matthew 28; 19, 20

> "Concerning His son, who was born of the seed of David according to the flesh, who was declared to be the Son of God with power, according to the spirit of holiness, by the resurrection from the dead, Yeshua the Messiah our Lord, through whom we received

---

[*] Appendix 3 at the end of this book on the Council of Nicaea

grace and apostleship, *to obedience of faith* among all the nations, for His name's sake."

—Romans 1:3-5

"Now to him that is able to establish you according to my gospel and the preaching of Yeshua the Messiah according to the revelation of the mystery which hath been kept in silence through times eternal, but now is manifested, and by the Scriptures of the prophets, *according to the commandment of the eternal God, is made known unto all the nations unto obedience of faith:* to the only wise God, through Yeshua, the Messiah to whom be the glory forever. Amen."

—*Romans* 16:25-27

The Key & the Secret for Life, Power, Authority, Miracles & Glory

"Most assuredly I tell you, he who believes in me, the works that I do, he will do also; and greater works than these will he do; because I am going to my father. Whatever you will ask in my name, that will I do, that the father may be glorified in the son. If you will ask anything in my name, that will I do. *If you love me, keep my commandments.*"

—John 14:12-15

CHAPTER ELEVEN
A Church Like Esther

"For if you altogether hold your peace at this time, then will relief and deliverance arise to the Jews from another place, but you and your father's house will perish: and who knows whether you haven't come to the kingdom for such a time as this?"
—Esther 4:14

By now it should be very clear that there are three factors that will keep us protected and sheltered during times of God's judgment and stormy weather,

1. Salvation and forgiveness of your sins through the blood atonement of Yeshua the Jewish Messiah on the execution stake (cross) in Jerusalem 2000 years ago, as stated in the Prophet Isaiah Chapter 53:

"Who has believed our message? And to whom has the arm of Yahveh been revealed? For He grew up before Him as a tender plant, and as a root out of a dry ground: He has no form nor comeliness; and when we see Him, there is no beauty that we should desire Him. He was despised, and rejected of men; a man of sorrows, and acquainted with grief: and as one from whom men hide their face He was despised; and we didn't respect Him. Surely He has borne our infirmities, and carried our sorrows; yet we esteemed Him stricken, struck of God, and afflicted. But He was wounded for our transgressions, He was bruised for our iniquities; the chastisement of our peace was on Him; and with His stripes we are healed. All we like sheep have gone astray; we have turned everyone to his own way; and Yahveh has laid on Him the iniquity of us all"

—Isaiah 53:1-6

And in the Book of John:

"For God so loved the world, that He gave His one and only Son, that whoever believes in Him should not perish, but have eternal life. For God didn't send His son into the world to judge the world, but that the world should be saved through Him. He who believes in Him is not judged. He who doesn't believe has been judged already because he has not believed in the name of the only born Son of God."

—John 3:15-18

2. Holiness and righteousness, obedience to God's Commandments

"The fear of Yahveh leads to life, then contentment; He rests and will not be touched by trouble."

—Proverbs 19:23

"It shall happen, if you shall listen diligently to the voice of Yahveh your God, to observe to do all His commandments which I command you this day, Yahveh your God will set you on high above all the nations of the earth: and all these blessings shall come on you, and overtake you, if you shall listen to the voice of Yahveh your God. Blessed shall you be in the city, and blessed shall you be in the field."

—Deuteronomy 28:1-3

"In the fear of Yahveh is a secure fortress, And He will be a refuge for His children. The fear of Yahveh is a fountain of life, turning people from the snares of death"

—Proverbs 14:26-27

"He who dwells in the secret place of the Most High will rest in the shadow of the Almighty. I will say of Yahveh, "He is my refuge and my fortress; My God, in whom I trust." For He will deliver you from the snare of the fowler, from the deadly pestilence. He will cover you with His pinions, Under His wings you will take refuge. His truth is a shield and a buckler. You will not be afraid of the terror by night, Nor of the arrow that flies by day; Nor of the pestilence that walks in darkness, Nor for the destruction that wastes at noonday. A thousand shall fall at your side, and ten thousand at your right hand; but it will not come near you. You will only look with your eyes, and see the reward of the wicked. For you, Yahveh, are my refuge! You have made the Most High your habitation. No evil will happen to you; neither shall any plague come near your tent. For He will give His angels charge over you, to guard you in all your ways. They will bear you up in their hands, so that you won't dash your foot against a stone. You will tread on the lion and cobra. You will trample the young lion and the serpent underfoot. Because He has set His love on me, therefore I will deliver him. I will set him on high because He has known my name. He will call on me, and I will answer him. I will be with him in trouble. I will deliver him, and honor him. I will satisfy him with long life, and show him my salvation."

—*Psalm 91*

3. A right relationship with Israel through blessing Israel and Yah's plan to restore His Jewish people in His covenant land as promised to Abraham.

In this chapter I will concentrate on the third point mentioned above - Our right relationship with Israel.

In order to do that I must introduce you to the key of Abraham; the key for you, your family and your nation to be blessed and protected even during the hard times; Moreover it is the key for the salvation of all the nations! Many nations are impenetrable to the Gospel because they have ignored and discarded this ancient key.

The Key of Abraham

> "I will bless those who bless you, and I will curse him who curses you. In you will all of the families of the earth be blessed."
>
> —*Genesis 12:3*

From the beginning the Creator appointed that His blessing and salvation to all the nations would come through one man – His chosen Abraham. The reason why He chose Abraham is the same reason by which He chose to save Noah and his family during the time of the great flood (Genesis 7) because Abraham was willing to follow Elohim and to keep His Commandments.

> And thus spoke the Almighty to Isaac, Abraham's son: "Sojourn in this land, and I will be with you, and will bless you. For to you, and to your seed, I will give all these lands, and I will establish the oath which I swore to Abraham your father. I will multiply your seed as the stars of the sky, and will give to your seed all these lands. In your seed will all the nations of the earth be blessed because *Abraham obeyed my voice, and kept my charge, my commandments, my statutes, and my laws.*" Isaac lived in Gerar."
>
> —*Genesis 26:3-6*

From then on, whoever would bless the natural seed and descendants would be blessed and prosper, and whoever would take them lightly, would be cursed and would suffer terrible consequences! We already touched on this thoroughly in Chapter Two, "For the Cause of Zion". By now you are thoroughly familiar with the fact that most of this stormy weather is happening in the earth because the nations have pressured Israel to give up her God-given covenant land to a brutal enemy that desires to destroy her and annihilate her all together.

Not many days ago, in this month of November, the Iranian president gave a public, hateful and virulent speech about the mandate of the Muslim nations to totally annihilate Israel. These speeches are not to be taken lightly. The late Yasser Arafat, the terrorist and murderer who was the father of the PLO and the ones called Palestinians today, (who were not a nation originally but have been made into a nation by the Muslim nations around Israel) gave many documented and well-recorded speeches about the plan to annihilate Israel through a peace by peace or piece by piece plan. Through coercion, political manipulation, lies and terror, they try to cause Israel to give up her land through a false peace process, piece by piece; until the whole land belongs to the Muslims and then Israel can be thrown out into the Mediterranean Sea... Again these are not words to be taken lightly! Especially since the Oslo accords and the infamous road map are already accomplishing these objectives. Terror in Israel and both terror and oil manipulation in the nations has been used by the USA, European and Far Eastern countries, to pressure Israel into giving up land and to evacuate precious citizens who have labored intensely for nearly 30 years to make sand dunes bloom! Today Israel has Jewish refugees from Gaza all over the land living in hotels. People of faith and sacrifice who provided jobs in their hothouses for their Arab neighbors until a day or two before the infamous disengagement! (I was there to see it with my own eyes! I could not believe that they trusted Yah to such an extent that they still had Muslims from Gaza and Khan Yunes working for them in spite of the danger of terror.)

There is a serious plan to destroy Israel again just like at the time of the Second World War when the Jews were expelled from Germany and marked for slaughter because they killed Jesus Christ.* But this time the plan is to destroy them in the name of the Muslim god Allah – who is not the God of Israel, whose name is Yah, not Allah. There are around six million Jews in Israel at present which is the same number of

---

* The Jews killed Christ - This is part of the infamous replacement theology that has caused the death of millions of Jews! The Jewish people had no jurisdiction to execute 2000 years ago, as they were under Rome. But even so, if Yeshua would have not died, there would be no blood atonement for sin and none could be saved. In any case both Jew and Gentile caused His death, as we all sinned and needed to be punished. Furthermore, Yeshua said: "Therefore the father loves me because I lay down my life, that I may take it again. No one takes it away from me, but I lay it down by myself. I have power to lay it down, and I have power to take it again. I received this commandment from my father." John 10:17,18

Jews that were exterminated during the Nazi Holocaust by the most Christian nation of its time, Germany!

Hitler quoted Martin Luther in his book Mein Kampf (My Struggle) and said that he was only following the words of the great reformer. The following are the words that Martin Luther wrote in his old age, in his book, "On the Jews and their Lies", after futile attempts to evangelize the Jewish people - who had been humiliated, tormented and massacred in the name of Christ since the Council of Nicaea in 325 AD. (twelve centuries by then!)

> "What shall we, Christians do with this damned rejected race of Jews? First, their synagogues should be set on fire. Secondly, their homes should likewise be broken down and destroyed (*Kristallnacht*). Thirdly, they should be deprived of their prayer books and Talmuds. Fourthly, their rabbis must be forbidden under threat of death to teach anymore. Fifthly, passports and traveling privileges should be absolutely forbidden to the Jews, let them stay at home (*ghettos*)... Let their young earn their bread by the sweat of their brow (*concentration camps*)... To sum up dear princes and nobles, who have Jews in your domains, if this advice of mine does not suit you, then find a better one (*death camps*) So that you and we may all be free of this insufferable, devilish burden – the Jews." (*final solution*) (Martin Luther, *On the Jews and their Lies*)

As Hitler followed the greatest Protestant reformer's instructions, he devised the hideous plan called "The Final Solution" by which he managed to exterminate, in gas chambers throughout conquered Poland, around six million Jews who were also burnt in ovens and crematoriums. The ashes of these Jews are still displayed in the Death Camps of Poland. A great mountain of them is clearly displayed in the death camp of Majdanek, not far from the city of Lublin in Poland.

Today there is again a plan to annihilate Israel. This time, not only by killing Jews that live outside of Israel but by destroying us in the Holy Land through the establishing of a Palestinian state - giving free access to armed terrorists on our roads without having a sound line of defense.

In view of this danger the Almighty is calling His church (His bride) to stand against this plan, like Mordechai of old called on Queen Esther to prevent that catastrophe. Queen Esther, who was a Jew and was married to the Persian king of her time, was afraid to obey Mordechai and intervene with her king in order to stop a wicked plan to annihilate the Jews of the Persian empire. However, Mordechai, her uncle who raised her as an orphan girl said these poignant words to her that resound throughout the ages:

> "For if you altogether hold your peace at this time, then will relief and deliverance arise to the Jews from another place, but you and your father's house will

perish: and who knows whether you haven't come to the kingdom for such a time as this?"

—Esther 4:14

In other words, if Queen Esther had decided not to intervene in this situation, the wicked plan of annihilation of the Jews would have eventually found her and killed her! For she was a Jew but she was a hidden Jew! That is what the name Esther means - *hidden*. *However, during the Nazi Holocaust, Hitler found all hidden Jews, even those who had converted* to Christianity - even those who were Jews from three or four generations back. They all went to the extermination camps!

The church is also like a 'hidden Jew', an Esther as she is grafted into the olive tree (Israel) through the blood of Yeshua and thus has become part of the Jewish people by blood covenant!

> "But if some of the branches were broken off, and you, *being a wild olive, were grafted in among them, and became partaker with them of the root of the richness of the olive tree;* don't boast over the branches. But if you boast, it is not you who bear the root, but the root you. You will say then: "Branches were broken off, that I might be grafted in." True; by their unbelief they were broken off, and you stand by your faith. Don't be conceited, but fear; for if God didn't spare the natural branches, neither will He spare you. See then the goodness and severity of God. Toward

those who fell, severity; but toward you, goodness, if you continue in His goodness; otherwise you also will be cut off."

—Romans 11:17-22

The enemy knows this, and so do the Muslims. They have spoken repeatedly of exterminating both Jews and Christians and in fact, about conquering the entire world. Whoever will allow the Jews to be harmed or exterminated, either by passive or active support of the PLO and the establishment of a Palestinian state in the land of Israel, will find themselves as targets of the same plan. This is why the USA, London, France, Belgium and many more countries are at the mercy of the Muslims who have been trained to kill in order to advance Islam. It is called Jihad - holy war in their Muslim jargon. The riots in France, the terror attacks on the underground of London, the explosions in the trains in Spain, the destruction of the Twin Towers in 9/11/2001 by Al Qaeda and much, much more is all part of the plan. In the Book of Obadiah, Yahveh warns all of us and all the nations:

> "For the day of Yahveh is near all the nations! As you have done, it will be done to you. Your deeds will return upon your own head. *For as you have drunk on my holy mountain, so will all the nations drink continually. Yes, they will drink, swallow down, and will be as though they had not been. But in Mount*

Zion, there will be those who escape, and it will be holy. The house of Jacob will possess their possessions."

—Obadiah 15-17

As you can see, the Almighty is promising that Israel will escape, but no other nation or person that does not stand by Israel has that promise. The only ones that are promised to be blessed and protected by Yah, are those who bless Israel and help her in the time of her distress:

"For the violence done to your brother Jacob, shame will cover you, and you will be cut off forever. In *the day that you stood on the other side,* in the day that strangers carried away his substance, and foreigners entered into his gates, and cast lots for Jerusalem, even you were like one of them."

—Obadiah 10-11

The nations and the church as a whole are all guilty before the Most High for allowing the Holocaust to happen during the Nazi regime. The entire world and the church stood "on the other side"; many of the Nazi executors were baptized Christians! Even worse than that, Martin Luther, the Protestant church father and reformer, was the inspiration for Hitler! Yah has given the church and the world sixty years of grace to recover from the Second World War but if the nations and most particularly the church will allow this hideous plan of extermination of Jews and the establishing of a Palestinian state, she will not be held guiltless before a holy God and she will suffer the same consequences!

Are you standing on the other side? Thinking that the plan to harm and annihilate Israel will not touch you? Are you too "politically correct"' to stand with Israel? Because you see, the enemies of Israel are also the enemies of God Himself!

"God, don't keep silent. Don't keep silent, and don't be still, God. For behold, your enemies are stirred up. Those who hate you have lifted up their heads. They conspire with cunning against your people. They plot against your cherished ones. "Come," they say, "and let us destroy them as a nation, that the name of Israel may be remembered no more." *For they have conspired together with one mind. They form an alliance against you. The tents of Edom and the Ishmaelites; Moab, and the Hagrites; Gebal, Ammon, and Amalek; Philistia with the inhabitants of Tyre; Assyria also is joined with them. They have helped the children of Lot. Selah. Do to them as you did to Midian, As to Sisera, as to Jabin, at the river Kishon; who perished at Endor, who became as dung for the earth. Make their nobles like Oreb and Zeeb; yes, all their princes like Zebah and Zalmunna; who said, "Let us take possession of God's pasturelands." My God, make them like tumbleweed; like chaff before the wind. As the fire that burns the forest, as the flame that sets the mountains on fire, so pursue them with your tempest, terrify them with your storm. Fill their faces with confusion, that they may seek your name, Yahveh. Let them be put to shame and dismayed forever. Yes, let them be confounded and perish; That they may know that you alone, whose name is Yahveh, are the Most High over all the earth" Psalm* 83

Queen Esther's response to the truth saved her life and the life of her people. If you and the church world-wide (beginning with you!) will respond in the same manner you will rescue your life, your family and maybe your nation:

> "Go, gather together all the Jews who are present in Shushan, and fast you for me, and neither eat nor drink three days, night or day: I also and my maidens will fast in like manner; and so will I go in to the king, which is not according to the law: and if I perish, I perish."
>
> —Esther 4:16

I would say to all of you my readers, go gather all your fellow believers, all your congregations, fast and pray for Israel like never before. Intervene with your national kings, priests, presidents, media men and women. Warn them about the wrath to come, tell them that there is more stormy weather ahead because the nations have touched the Apple of Yah's eye - Israel. Call them to repent and to stop pushing Israel to the Mediterranean Sea by establishing a terrorist Palestinian state in her midst. Tell them to stop funding terror; because what they sow they reap, that is why terror is running rampant in the streets of the nations... And the worst is yet to come. Plead with them; warn them that much stormy weather is still ahead.

But for those who will protect Israel at this time, there will be signs and wonders of protection and blessing in the midst of judgment, just as He promised;

An Esther kind of church full of authority will arise and attain much power and glory and bring forth the End Time harvest of the nations!

> "I will bless those who bless you, and I will curse him who curses you. In you will all of the families of the earth be blessed."
>
> —Genesis 12:3

Make it a point to pray for Israel and for the shalom, the well-being of Jerusalem every day; even before you pray for your own needs and begin to see Yah move on your behalf.

> "Pray for the peace of Jerusalem. They will prosper who love you. Peace be within your walls, and prosperity within your palaces. For my brothers' and companions' sakes, I will now say, "Peace be within you."
>
> —Psalm 122:6-8

A recent story came into our hands from some of our precious friends in the USA. They are contractors and builders and one of their customers gave them a bad check that bounced. That caused a domino effect and the cement company that supplied them had their check bounce as well. Because of this, the cement company closed their account and paralyzed our friend's business. This situation brought them to the edge of disaster, as they could build no more houses! The wife reminded her husband about the key of Abraham - bless Israel, pray for the peace of Jerusalem first. So, they both began to pray for Jerusalem and Israel. Then she said: Call the cement company, apologize, explain what happened and beg for mercy. The cement company manager came back to them and said: "I don't know why we are doing this, as we have never done this before, but we are going to give you a second chance" - Thus they reopened their cement account and their business was rescued! Praise Yah for His Word is true! We have heard many stories like this one! Yah is waiting to bless you and to bail you out of impossible situations... if you just put Israel first. If you are just willing to stand with the Apple of His eye, Israel - in spite of their unbelief Yah loves them and has chosen them forever!

> "If I forget you, Jerusalem, Let my right hand forget its skill. Let my tongue stick to the roof of my mouth, if I don't remember you; if I don't prefer Jerusalem above my chief joy."
>
> —Psalm 137:5-6

An Important Prayer

Yes Father, I answer the call to be like Esther and stand on behalf of Israel. I will not stand on 'the other side' and if I perish, I perish. I take the risk to be misunderstood and even hated by Your enemies. I choose to be Your friend in this End Time and a friend of the people and the land that you have chosen - Israel. Thank you for blessing me and my family, and for protecting me as you promised in Your word. I will pray for the peace and well-being of Jerusalem first - thank you that you will take care of my other needs. In Yeshua's name. Amen!

CHAPTER TWELVE
True Leadership for Stormy Weather

"There shall not any man be able to stand before you all the days of your life. As I was with Moses, so I will be with you; I will not fail you, nor forsake you. Be strong and of good courage; for you shall cause these people to inherit the land, which I swore to their fathers to give them. Only be strong and very courageous, to observe to do according to all the law, which Moses my servant commanded you: don't turn from it to the right hand or to the left, that you may have good success wherever you go. This book of the law shall not depart out of your mouth, but you shall meditate thereon day and night, that you may observe to do according to all that is written therein: for then you shall make your way prosperous, and then you shall have good success. Haven't I commanded you? Be strong and of good courage; don't be afraid, neither be dismayed: for Yahveh your God is with you wherever you go."
—Joshua 1:5-9

The following stories touched my heart as they show the marks of true courage and leadership. These two may have not known God but they displayed His commandment- "Love your neighbor as yourself" and,

> "Greater love has no one than this, that a man lay down his life for his friends."
>
> —John 15:13

Andrew 'Ned' Kelly and Nick Ward, from Stourbridge, West Midlands, had been planning to leave Phi Phi island when the tsunami hit.

Instead, they lowered themselves from their hotel room to a nearby rooftop and began dragging people from the water surging past them.

The pair saved as many as 50 people, despite the threat of further waves and the presence of high-voltage power cables near their position.

They then started treating the injured in their hotel room, using bed linen to bandage wounds.

After hearing that a second impact was expected, they carried the injured to the second floor of the hotel.

The following day they helped carry people, using improvised stretchers, to helicopters or boats waiting to take casualties to hospital.

But the men reject any suggestion their actions were "heroic". "I see myself as a lucky survivor who was in a position where I could help people," said 38-year-old Mr. Kelly, a West Midlands police sergeant.

Mr. Ward, a 35-year-old engraver, added: "It's just what anybody would do. I just did as much as I could".

A Swedish tourist who was pictured running into the Asian tsunami to save her family, survived the catastrophe, as did her children.

Newspapers around the world showed a desperate Karin Svaerd heading into the waves as other tourists fled.

On Sunday the 37-year-old policewoman told the press she survived by grabbing hold of a palm tree on the Thai beach.

But it was an agonizing ten minutes before she discovered that her husband and three children had also escaped.

"I can remember the white foam, how the surf took them up and they disappeared," she told Britain's News of the World in an interview published on Sunday. Witnesses said she screamed: "Oh my God, not my children!"

"I could hear people shouting at me 'Get off the beach' as I ran past them - but I ignored them," she said.

"I had to try and save my children, nothing was going to stop me."

She said she thought she would die as she was engulfed by the tide, but in fact it swept her onto higher ground at the resort of Krabi.

Then she feared for her husband Lars, her sons Anton, 14, Filip, 11, and Viktor, 10, and her brother, Per.

She found them together ten minutes later.

They flew back to Sweden, arriving on 30 December, and saw the pictures in the press, under headlines like: "No one knows if they survived."

"Now, our family is closer than ever before," Mrs. Svaerd said. "We came so close to death that we realize how valuable life is."

What kind of leaders do we need in light of all these shakings and storms? We need courageous, fearless, well-grounded and well-equipped leaders who can both rescue and train their people in how to behave during storms. Notice that in both the above stories the rescuers were police people, one a man and the other a woman. The police are assigned to keep and restore order, to punish the wicked and to rescue the endangered. Policemen enforce the *law and are trained to act in times of crisis. All End Time leaders should also be law enforcers and well trained to act in times of* crisis.

These leaders will be like Joshua, courageous men and women who fear Yah alone. They will be solid in their foundation and will meditate in the law of God day and night, not only on His promises but also especially on His laws and Commandments. Most of the leaders today do not qualify to be leaders during times of storms. The best of them are telling their people to meditate on God's promises but almost none encourage their people to meditate on Yahveh's laws and Commandments. It is meditation and obedience to *His eternal laws and Commandments that bring about prosperity and success* even in times of great shaking and storms. Most of the promises of the Most High are conditional on our obedience to Him. It is those that fear Him who will be protected during the hard times.

> "Because you kept the word of my patience, I also will keep you from the hour of testing, that which is to come on the whole world, to test those who dwell on the earth."
>
> —Revelation 3:10

It is not enough to be well meaning. The world needs a leadership that knows the ways of the Almighty in the Storms. Far too many leaders have the fear of man and are caressing the ears of their flocks. Unless they repent they will be judged severely.

> "Let not many of you be teachers, my brothers, knowing that we will receive heavier judgment."
>
> —Yaacov (James) 3:1

> "I charge you therefore before God and the Lord, Yeshua the Messiah, who will judge the living and the dead at His appearing and His Kingdom: preach the word; be urgent in season and out of season; reprove, rebuke, and exhort, with all patience and teaching. For the time will come when they will not listen to the sound doctrine, but, having itching ears, will heap up for themselves teachers after their own lusts; and will turn away their ears from the truth, and turn aside to fables. But you be sober in all things, suffer

hardship, do the work of an evangelist, and fulfill your ministry."
—2 Timothy 4:1-5

There are too many soothsayers who call themselves prophets and apostles who are not warning the church or the nations of the judgment to come. They are ostracizing those who are sounding a warning with a clear shofar blow that Yeshua is returning soon and that we all need to repent and prepare.

> "Again, when a righteous man does turn from his righteousness, and commit iniquity, and I lay a stumbling block before him, he shall die: because you have not given him warning, he shall die in his sin, and his righteous deeds which he has done shall not be remembered; but his blood will I require at your hand. Nevertheless, if you warn the righteous man, that the righteous not sin, and he does not sin, he shall surely live, because he took warning; and you have delivered your soul."
> —Ezekiel 3:20-21

There are many soothsayers who are explaining away the judgments of God, based on their wrong theology, saying that He is too good to judge His own people. Go tell that to my people Israel! And go tell that lie to Ananias and Saphiras who died in the Presence of the Almighty for lying to the Holy Spirit on a matter of finances (Acts 5). Also try to convince Yeshua our master who tells us clearly in the Book of Revelation:

> "To the angel of the assembly in Laodicea write: "The amen, the faithful and true witness, the head of God's creation, says these things: "I know your works, that you are neither cold nor hot. I wish you were cold or hot. So, because you are lukewarm, and neither hot nor cold, I will vomit you out of my mouth. Because you say, 'I am rich, and have gotten riches, and have need of nothing;' and don't know that you are the wretched one, miserable, poor, blind, and naked; I counsel you to buy from me gold refined by fire, that you may become rich; and white garments, that you may clothe yourself, and that the shame of your nakedness may not be revealed; and eye salve to anoint your eyes, that you may see. As many as I love, I reprove and chasten. Be zealous therefore, and repent."
>
> —Revelation 3:14-19

Or when He speaks to us the following about Himself:

> "Don't be afraid of those who kill the body, but are not able to kill the soul. Rather, fear Him who is able to destroy both soul and body in Gehenna"
>
> —Matthew 10:28

Let me paraphrase this for you: "Do not fear men who persecute you or any demon but fear Me, the only one that has the power to send you to hell"

That is not very nice and yet it is true! He still retains the power of judgment and He is still saying to the church what He said to Israel 2,000 years ago:

> But when He saw many of the Pharisees and Sadducees coming for His baptism, He said to them, "You offspring of vipers, who warned you to flee from the wrath to come? *Therefore bring forth fruit worthy of repentance!* Don't think to yourselves, 'We have Abraham for our father', for I tell you that God is able to raise up children to Abraham from these stones. Even now the axe lies at the root of the trees. Therefore, every tree that doesn't bring forth good fruit is cut down, and cast into the fire. I indeed baptize you in water for repentance, but He who comes after me is mightier than I, whose shoes I am not worthy to carry. He shall baptize you in the Holy Spirit. His winnowing fork is in His hand, and He will thoroughly cleanse His threshing with unquenchable fire."
>
> —Matthew 3:7-12

In other words do not say: "I am a Christian, I have the blood of Jesus". The Blood of Yeshua is not a 'lucky charm', it is the most precious commodity ever purchased! And if you do have His blood then you cannot reject His laws and Commandments and stay in sin any longer. There are no excuses for immorality, idolatry, witchcraft and disobedience.

The true leaders of this Millennium will be filled with holy compassion and will confront the sin in the church, will cast out devils, teach Torah and His laws, heal the sick and more than anything will show an example of Godliness in their own lives! They will be Yah's policemen and will restore order, respect for the laws of the Creator and will rescue many.

God's true leaders are examples which the flock can follow! Far from being perfect they are constantly being perfected; they are disciplined in their lifestyle and they always bear in mind that they represent the Almighty. They are truly aware of their weakness but are so dependent on the Holy Spirit that in their weaknesses Yah is made strong. They will come from all backgrounds and all walks of life, but they would have departed thoroughly from sin and evil. They are truthful, honest and transparent, shunning all hidden sin. They are full of holy fire and passion for Yeshua and His people. They are creative, non-rigid and yet disciplined and holy from the inside out – full of anointing and the glory of Yah is clearly seen upon them. The holy angels of Yah are constantly working with them, so they command respect and the holy fear of Yah!

They are constantly willing to be transformed by Him, are obedient and teach obedience, are quick to repent and to forgive. They are humble and yet fearsome, compassionate and yet full of authority. If you meet one of them you know that you are in the presence of a true leader! Many of the young people of today will be like young King Josiah (2 Kings 22) and will become such passionate, holy leaders that they will command respect!

Only a holy and sacrificial leadership, full of Yah's authority will be able to navigate the church in times of "Stormy Weather".

> "Those who are wise shall shine as the brightness of the expanse; and those who turn many to righteousness as the stars forever and ever."
> —Daniel 12:3

> 'The fear of Yahveh is the beginning of wisdom; a good understanding have all they that do [His commandments]: His praise endureth forever."
> —Psalm 111:10 Standard Version

All the other ones who are so puffed up with their own selfish ambition, self-importance, self-indulgence and compromise will not be able to make it. The smallest storms will cause them to stumble and with them their flocks will stumble too. It is time to repent, church; and first of all the pastors, the leaders, the prophets, the teachers... There is simply no other way than to return to the original Hebrew foundations which the Jewish Apostles had. We have a lot to unlearn from 1600 years of divorce* from the original foundations of the church and a whole lot to learn. Only remember that by the grace of God you are reading this book today. It may not be 'elegantly written' or 'hermeneutically perfect' but it is *truth*.

There is a spiritual tsunami coming, the waters of past revivals have receded and the foundations of the church have been uncovered and they are faulty - they need to be replaced with the original, ancient everlasting foundations.

There is no time for 'niceties'. We need to repent quickly before it's too late! In 1996 Yah spoke to me that it is a matter of life and death for the church to return to the Jewish roots of the Faith and now it is 2005! Many have been dying on the vine or leaving their churches; many are in confusion and try to calm the masses with more entertainment.

Seek God! Repent! Be cleansed and sanctified. A spiritual tsunami is on the way! Revival is on the way, but if your foundations are wrong it cannot withstand the force of Yah's glory - His kavod (from the word weighty or heavy in Hebrew). Many are praying for revival and Adonai is saying - Repent and return to the original foundations, let Me change you!

The true leaders of this End Time revival must go through this repentance-transformation-restoration process. That is why we bring people to Israel to train them quickly before the coming revival 'hits'. Even though Israel as a nation is in sin for the most part and needs to repent also; the Hebrew

---

* Read Appendix at the end of this book on the Council of Nicaea

Holy Scriptures are spotless and still remain our standard for life. Yah is still using Israel and Jerusalem to train the nations in His ways:[*]

> "The word that Isaiah the son of Amoz saw concerning Judah and Jerusalem. It shall happen in the latter days, that the mountain of Yahveh's house shall be established on the top of the mountains, and shall be raised above the hills; and all nations shall flow to it. Many peoples shall go and say, Come you, and let us go up to the mountain of Yahveh, to the house of the God of Jacob; and He will teach us of His ways, and we will walk in His paths: for out of Zion shall go forth the law and the word of Yahveh from Jerusalem."
>
> —Isaiah 2:1-3

---

[*] Concerning our End time leadership training sessions in Israel please contact us through www.kad-esh.org or info@kad-esh.org

CLOSURE
Half an Hour of Prayer & Silence

"When He opened the seventh seal, there followed a silence in heaven for about half an hour. I saw the seven angels who stand before God, and seven trumpets were given to them."
—Revelation 8:1

Another angel came and stood over the altar, having a golden censer. Much incense was given to him, that he should add it to the prayers of all the saints on the golden altar, which was before the throne. The smoke of the incense, with the prayers of the saints, went up before God out of the angel's hand. The angel took the censer, and he filled it with the fire of the altar, and threw it on the earth. There followed thunders, sounds, lightning, and an earthquake. The seven angels who had the seven trumpets prepared themselves to sound. The first sounded, and there followed hail and fire, mingled with blood, and they were thrown on the earth. One third of the earth was burnt up, and one third of the trees were burnt up, and all green grass was burnt up. The second angel sounded, and something like a great mountain burning with fire was thrown into the sea. One third of the sea became blood, and one third of the creatures which were in the sea died, those who had life. One third of the ships were destroyed. The third angel sounded, and a great star fell from the sky, burning like a torch, and it fell on one third of the rivers, and on the springs of the waters. The name of the star is called "Wormwood." One third of the waters became wormwood. Many men died from the waters because they were made bitter. The fourth angel sounded, and one third of the sun was struck, and one third of the moon, and one third of the stars; so that one third of them would be darkened, and the day wouldn't shine for one third of it, and the night in the same way. I saw, and I heard an eagle, flying in mid heaven, saying with a loud voice, "Woe! Woe! Woe for those who dwell on the earth, because of the other voices of the trumpets of the three angels, who are yet to sound."

—Revelation 8:2-13

When I first came to Yoido's Prayer Mountain in South Korea in 1993, I went into one of the prayer grottos that look like little tombs or burial caves on the side of the mountain. The moment I got in, the spirit of prayer fell on me powerfully! Half an hour later I had prayed through and could pray no more. My husband went into one of the prayer caves and it took him one and a half hours until he had his breakthrough. This year, as I was writing this book, I went every day to pray at around 3 pm, into one of the prayer grottos and the same thing happened to me every day. I began to pray and half an hour later I was done and could pray no more. This happened every day without fail! I began to wonder what it meant, when Rev. Daniel Flueckiger, my intercessor and armor-bearer pointed me to the half-hour silence in Heaven prior to the outpouring of Yah's judgment and wrath on the earth and its inhabitants.

Then I realized that my half an hour daily intercession represented the last bit of grace prior to the half hour of silence that precedes His full judgment. The silence of the Almighty always represents His judgment.

This book is also a fruit of my half-hour prayers of intercession on behalf of the church and the nations. I am not just anyone; I am a Jew. At the hands of the nations and most particularly the church in the nations (in years past), my people have suffered death and destruction from pogroms, the Spanish Inquisition, the Nazi Holocaust and many other humiliations.

Today we are suffering at the hands of an anti-Semitic world; politics coming from the USA, the European Union, the United Nations, the World Council of Churches, Russia, the World Bank, the Muslim nations and more. Yahveh is using this Jewish woman to write this book as an act of grace for both the church and the nations. This book has come into your hands to provoke you to repent, accept the blood sacrifice of Yeshua the Messiah on behalf of your sins and to be restored to the fear of Yah by obeying His Commandments. It is the same for you if you are a Jew, a Gentile, a Moslem or a Christian. If you neglect to repent, listen to these eternal words of warning written by Shaul-Paul, the Jewish apostle to the gentiles nearly 2000 years ago,

> "According to your hardness and impenitent heart you are treasuring up for yourself wrath in the day of wrath and revelation of the righteous judgment of God; who "will render to every man according to his works:" to those who by patience in well-doing seek for glory and honor and incorruptibility, eternal life; but to those who are self-seeking, and don't obey the truth, but obey unrighteousness, will be wrath and indignation, oppression and anguish, on every soul of man who works evil, on the Jew first, and also on the Greek. But glory and honor and peace to every man who works good, to the Jew first, and also to the Greek. For there is no partiality with God. For as many as have sinned without law will also perish without the law. As many as have sinned under the law will be judged by the law. For it isn't the hearers of the law who are righteous before God, but the doers of the law will be justified"
>
> —Romans 2:5-13

Much stormy weather is still ahead of us and only those who fear Yahveh will be saved and rescued, both through these rough times and for eternity. They will become renowned men and women filled with glory, cooperating with the holy angels of Yah and bringing in the great harvest of the End Times! They will be followed by the most astounding signs, wonders and miracles the world has ever seen.

I pray that you, my reader will be one of them.

"I lifted up my eyes, and saw, and behold, a man with a measuring line in His hand. Then said I, Where go you? He said to me, to measure Jerusalem, to see what is the breadth of it, and what is the length of it. Behold, the angel who talked with me went forth, and another angel went out to meet him, and said to him, Run, speak to this young man, saying, Jerusalem shall be inhabited as villages without walls, by reason of the multitude of men and cattle therein. For I, says Yahveh, will be to her a wall of fire round about, and I will be the glory in the midst of her. Ho, ho, flee from the land of the north, says Yahveh; for I have spread you abroad as the four winds of the sky, says Yahveh. Ho Zion, escape, you who dwell with the daughter of Babylon. For thus says Yahveh of hosts: After glory has he sent me to the nations, which plundered you; for he who touches you touches the apple of His eye. For, behold, I will shake my hand over them, and they shall be a spoil to those who served them;

and you shall know that Yahveh of Hosts has sent me. Sing and rejoice, daughter of Zion; for behold, I come, and I will dwell in the midst of you, says Yahveh. Many nations shall join themselves to Yahveh in that day, and shall be my people; and I will dwell in the midst of you, and you shall know that Yahveh of Hosts has sent me to you. Yahveh shall inherit Judah as His portion in the holy land, and shall yet choose Jerusalem. Be silent, all flesh, before Yahveh; for He is waked up out of His holy habitation."

—Zechariah 2:1-13*

---

*   I strongly suggest that you follow up this reading with my foundations trilogy; "The Healing Power of the Roots", "Sheep Nations" and "Grafted In", so you know how to live, follow and serve the Creator in order to be empowered by His Spirit, favored and protected by Him during these times of stormy weather.

APPENDIX A
Current Events

The following update is taken from Bill Koenig's web page. Please subscribe to his page to continue updating yourself as more events unfold. Visit www.watch.org to subscribe.

Why are some Christian leaders not taking a stand for Israel's biblical right to all of Judea and Samaria, instead facilitating the dream of an Arab state in the biblical heartland of Israel?

For some reason, a few Christians believe they have a responsibility to be ardent backers of Israel-Arab normalizations at the expense of Israel and her settlement communities. This has motivated them to attempt to influence the Trump Administration and Israel's public opinion accordingly.

They were also strong supporters of President Trump's Peace to Prosperity Plan and greatly encouraged Jared Kushner the architect of the plan. Furthermore, they won't acknowledge the extreme difference in life in America before January 28, 2020, when the Trump plan was introduced at the White House, and the corresponding COVID-19 pandemic in the United States and Israel.

One of them even blamed PM Netanyahu for the COVID-19 crisis and lockdown for taking his "eye off the ball" during his annexation efforts (we prefer extended sovereignty efforts). Why does he keep calling it annexation? Secretary of State Mike Pompeo calls it extended sovereignty and so does Ambassador David Friedman.

Do they realize the normalization efforts they are supporting with the Arabs are setting the path for the peace deal of the Antichrist?

We need to continue to stand for God's covenant land and not support agreements that will become or lead to the Antichrist's deal of Daniel 9:27 (which is inevitable at some point). Supporting those agreements continues the confusion over whose land Judea and Samaria is. (Below is my direct confrontation of the ELCA Isaiah 58 leadership over whose land it is.)

The Bible says this in Joel 3:2: "I will also gather all nations, and will bring them down into the valley of Jehoshaphat, and will plead with them there for my people and for my heritage Israel, whom they have scattered among the nations, and parted my land" (KJV).

Practical approach taken over biblical approach by Israeli governments

An Israeli official told me this many years ago after I spoke of the consequences of dividing the biblical land of Israel: "There is a biblical view and there is a practical view. We prefer to take the practical view."

I have told my Jewish friends and acquaintances over the years that they will not have peace until the Prince of Peace—Yeshua—returns. I tell them they all long for peace to the point they are willing to compromise in land negotiations, but they won't have peace until they call on His name and He returns.

Five main problems with the Abraham Accords that Christians shouldn't support

- The Abraham Accords stop Israel's rightful plan to extend sovereignty. The United Arab Emirates said they were told no annexation discussions until 2024 or later. This week at the U.N. the UAE Foreign Minister Sheikh Abdullah bin Zayed stated two states based on pre-1967 lines, meaning almost all of Judea and Samaria. He said normalization was done to stop Israeli annexation.

- Moreover, this leaves 132 settlement communities and 12 Jewish enclaves in the state of flux after Netanyahu promises, not knowing if Trump will be re-elected. Plus, Ambassador Friedman said this week that sovereignty efforts could be revisited in a year while Kushner continues to push that date off— if ever. Kushner is determined to do more normalization deals and doesn't want annexation to get in the way. His justification is that no one (settler) will be forced from their home.

- The Abraham Accords acknowledged the U.N. in sections 8, 9 and 12. This keeps the U.N. in a central role and gives the 54 Muslim nations and others in the U.N. the opportunity to continually pass biased anti-Israel resolutions, etc.

- The Abraham Accords continued the two-state narrative. In the last two weeks every Middle East Sunni country stated in their annual U.N. General Assembly messages their full backing of the Arab Peace Initiative of 2002 based on pre-1967 lines.

- The Abraham Accords has revived, elevated and legitimized the Arab Peace Initiative of 2002 to the most acceptable Sunni plan, which is based on U.N. Resolutions 242 and 338. It calls for Palestinian refugees to be relocated to a future Palestinian state.

US Sponsored Abraham Accords First Meeting and Hurricane Delta

Weather Channel: Atlantic Basin quiet for almost 2 months until Tropical Depression 26 forms on Sunday afternoon, October 4, becoming Hurricane Delta the afternoon of October 6

Hurricane seasons calmed: On Saturday, September 26, the Weather Channel stated the Atlantic Basin hurricane was blank for the first time in almost 2 months. That no tropical formation was expected in the next five days. On Sunday, October 4 the storm that became Hurricane Delta began as a tropical depression.

Tuesday, October 6, 2020

US Sponsored Abraham Accords First Meeting Tuesday: Israeli, UAE foreign ministers meet in Berlin, which is 'honored' to host summit - Times of Israel

The foreign ministers of the United Arab Emirates and Israel were meeting in Berlin on Tuesday for talks that Germany hopes will strengthen the nascent official ties between the two nations and bolster broader Middle East peace efforts in a summit that

Foreign Minister Heiko Maas said it was a "great honor" to host.

Foreign Minister Gabi Ashkenazi and Emirati Foreign Minister Sheikh Abdullah bin Zayed Al Nahyan were to meet, along with Maas, behind closed doors at a secluded government guesthouse on the outskirts of the German capital.

While the two have spoken over the phone, this will be the first public meeting between the two senior officials.

Maas said it was a "great honor that the Israeli and Emirati foreign ministers have chosen Berlin as the location for their historic first meeting" since the two countries agreed to normalize relations in a US-brokered deal.

Maas said the "courageous peace agreement" between the two countries is "the first good news from the Mideast in a long time, and at the same time an opportunity for new movement in the dialogue between Israel and the Palestinians."

Germany is a strong supporter of Israel, but at the same time has been critical of its settlement policies and also works closely with the Palestinians and is in favor of a Palestinian state as part of a two state solution.

Abraham Accords: Trump announces Israel-Sudan Deal and Hurricane Zeta

Abraham Accords timeline: Zeta began 25 hours after President Trump's introduction of the Israel-Sudan deal and VP Pence's chief of staff and four others tested positive for COVID-19

NHC: Hurricane Zeta: Storm began Sat. at 5pm ET, 25 hours after Trump announcement of Israel-Sudan deal

OCTOBER 23, 2020

With Netanyahu on phone, euphoric Trump predicts 'one unified family' in Mideast.

OCTOBER 23, 2020

Trump announces Israel-Sudan peace deal, has call with Netanyahu, Sudan leaders.

OCTOBER 23, 2020

America hits highest daily number of coronavirus cases since pandemic began.

OCTOBER 24, 2020

Mossad head: Saudi normalization ties to be announced after US election.

OCTOBER 25, 2020

Billboards blame Jared, Ivanka for COVID-19 response, spark legal battle.

OCTOBER 25, 2020

US sees record 88,973 Covid-19 infections for second day straight.

OCTOBER 25, 2020

Pence's chief of staff, Marc Short, tests positive for the coronavirus.

OCTOBER 25, 2020

5 close to Pence test positive for coronavirus, VP to maintain campaign schedule, office says.

OCTOBER 28, 2020

Hurricane Zeta Rapidly Strengthens Into Category 2 as it Nears Landfall in Louisiana, Mississippi.

OCTOBER 28, 2020

Friedman: US-Israel 'righting old wrongs' by extending W. Bank agreements; but not sovereignty.

Netanyahu fetes 'important victory' as US okays funding science projects in settlements.

OCTOBER 28, 2020

Hurricane Zeta makes landfall on Louisiana coast as Category 2 storm; 1 mph under Category 3.

Hurricane Delta major intensification to Category 4 the afternoon of October 6.

Abraham Accords Chronology for the Week: Trump announces Israel-Sudan deal, 7.5 Alaska quake and COVID crisis worsens.

OCTOBER 19, 2020

Trump to drop Sudan from terror list in presumed prelude to Israel normalization.

OCTOBER 19, 2020

USGS: 7.5 Alaska Quake - 91 km SE of Sand Point, Alaska; multiple 4 and 5 magnitude aftershocks continue.

OCTOBER 23, 2020

Trump announces Israel-Sudan peace deal, has call with Netanyahu, Sudan leaders - Times of Israel

We are praying that Israel-Sudan normalization agreement announced today won't be costly to President Trump. His team forced this through and even took Sudan off the terror list after they agreed to pay $335 million in compensation to the victims of the 1998 bombings of two US Embassies in Africa (The Times of Israel said Sudan didn't perpetrate the attacks, which killed more than 4,000 people, but granted asylum to the terrorists)

The Times of Israel reported together with a massive financial aid package for the struggling country — the US has reportedly offered $800 million in aid and investments, but Sudan demands some $3-4 billion — the removal of the terrorism designation is largely seen as a precursor to a normalization deal with Israel.

US Health Experts Projecting Major Exponential Increase in COVID Cases

At the same time, U.S. health experts are projecting a major exponential increase in COVID cases next week. Former FDA Director Scott Dr. Scott Gottlieb: U.S. about 'a week away from a rapid acceleration' of coronavirus cases - CNBC.

Thursday and Friday of this week both had 70,000 plus new cases reported.

Abraham Accords: US weapon sale to UAE and Hurricane Eta

Abraham Accord timeline: US weapon sale to UAE and Hurricane Eta

On November 7 morning, Eta regained Tropical Storm strength in the Caribbean Sea. Tropical Storm warnings were issued for South Florida and the Florida keys. This was after a strong hit on Honduras. The actions and paths of this storm were very unusual.*

NOVEMBER 7, 2020

Trump administration advances $10 billion defense sale to UAE.

NOVEMBER 7, 2020

Tropical Storm Eta Crossing Cuba; Storm Surge, Hurricane Watches Issued for Florida.

NOVEMBER 7, 2020

Tropical Storm Eta is formed.

NOVEMBER 10, 2020

Pompeo announces $23b sale of F-35s, other arms to UAE, links it to Israel peace.

NOVEMBER 11, 2020

Eta Strengthens Into a Hurricane Off Southwest Coast of Florida.

---

* https://www.nhc.noaa.gov/archive/2020/ETA.shtml?

NOVEMBER 12, 2020

Eta's second Florida landfall floods cities, traps dozens in cars and homes.

APPENDIX C
A Recount on Replacement Theology

The reason Jewish roots were lost early in church history is because our revered church fathers were antisemitic, deliberately changing Jewish celebrations and altering some doctrines to make a complete break from Judaism. In the second century, Justin Martyr, Polycarp, and Marcion were among those beginning the onslaught against the Jewish people and Judaism. Marcion in the middle of the second century was the first to write that the New Covenant had replaced all previous covenants - and he was known as a heretic. His writing was later taken seriously and led to replacement theology, the elements of which show up in the Thompson Chain-Reference Bible. On the back of the New Testament title page there is a chart listing contrasts between the Old and New Testaments including spiritual darkness vs. light of world, death reigns vs. life eternal and fifteen others. Jesus and His disciples would not agree with that chart. Jesus said, "Do not think that I came to abolish the Torah... (Matthew 5:17-20)

In the fourth century, John Chrysostom, known for powerful, eloquent sermons, gave a series of seventeen virulently anti-Semitic sermons at a time when the pagan celebration of Ishtar (Easter), the fertility goddess, was set to replace Passover for the celebration of Jesus' death and resurrection. Also, the Roman winter solstice celebration, in honor of the god Saturn, was established as the celebration of Jesus' birth. In the fifth century Augustine brought Greek philosophy into Christian theology, which has influenced the church to this day.j

The celebrations introduced in the fourth century put a seal on the separation from Judaism and set the stage for violence against the Jewish people. Jewish people even today often view Christians as "the enemy" and with good reason. Over the centuries Christians have outperformed all other groups combined in the killing of Jews. There were numerous pogroms throughout Europe from early on through to the Holocaust. In medieval Spain children at the age of eight were taken from Jewish parents to be raised in Christian homes. Jews were frequently forced to convert to Christianity, and afterward were still persecuted for being Jewish. In 1492, Ferdinand and Isabella forced the Jews to leave Spain. Such forced exoduses were common, with Jews moving from one country to another, virtually all over Europe. Every

European country expelled Jews at least once. Jews were forbidden to own land until they came to the American colonies. The Spanish Inquisition is well known for cruelty to the Jews.

The Holocaust was not the end of antisemitism and not the sole evidence of it in WW II. During the Holocaust not one Christian denomination spoke out against the attempted extermination of the Jewish people. The US government turned away a ship loaded with Jewish refugees from Europe and forced it to return to Europe to certain death for the passengers. US bombers flew over Auschwitz nearly every night to bomb railroad marshalling yards just a few miles away, but never bombed the gas chambers, seemingly to "avoid possible collateral damage, killing or injuring prisoners" who were going to be gassed in the very near future. Today, antisemitism is rising throughout the world, especially in Europe. It is very strong at the UN.

To understand the Jewish roots of Christianity, look first to the Hebrew Scriptures. Among the first things the early church did to divorce from Judaism was changing the seasons of the Lord. These are detailed in Leviticus 23, beginning with the Sabbath. The church at Constantine's behest moved Jesus' death and resurrection from Passover and introduced Easter, then added Christmas to celebrate Jesus' birth.

His birth, death, and resurrection certainly need to be honored, but not with pagan holidays.

As the church returns to its Jewish Roots it is not to copy modern Judaism, to be pretend Jews. The church needs to study Scripture, honoring the commandments that have been forsaken, becoming worshipers in spirit and in truth." (Rev. Bill Moreford, "The Seasons of the Lord")

APPENDIX D
Revocation of the Council of Nicaea

From the letter of the Emperor (Constantine) to all those not present at the council. (Found in Eusebius, Vita Const., Lib III 18-20)

When the question relative to the sacred festival of Easter arose, it was universally thought that it would be convenient that all should keep the feast on one day; for what could be more beautiful and more desirable than to see this festival, through which we receive the hope of immortality, celebrated by all with one accord and in the same manner? It was declared to be particularly unworthy for this, the holiest of festivals, to follow the customs (the calculation) of the Jews who had soiled their hands with the most fearful of crimes, and whose minds were blinded. In rejecting their custom we may transmit to our descendants the legitimate mode of celebrating Easter; which we have observed from the time of the Saviour's passion (according to the day of the week).

We ought not, therefore, to have anything in common with the Jew, for the Saviour has shown us another way; our worship following a more legitimate and more convenient course (the order of the days of the week: And consequently in unanimously adopting this mode, we desire, dearest brethren to separate ourselves from the detestable company of the Jew. For it is truly shameful for us to hear them boast that without their direction, we could not keep this feast. How can they be in the right, they who, after the death of the Saviour, have no longer been led by reason but by wild violence, as their delusion may urge them? They do not possess the truth in this Easter question, for in their blindness and repugnance to all improvements they frequently celebrate two Passovers in the same year. We could not imitate those who are openly in error.

How, then, could we follow these Jews who are most certainly blinded by error? For to celebrate a Passover twice in one year, is totally inadmissible.

But even if this were not so it would still be your duty not to tarnish your soul by communication with such wicked people (the Jews). You should consider not only that the number of churches in these provinces make a majority, but also that it is right to demand what our reason approves, and that we should have nothing in common with the Jews. (Gleaned from Dr. Henry R. Percival's *"The Nicaean and Post Nicaean Fathers."* Vol. XIV Grand Rapid: Erdmans pub. 1979, pgs. 54-55)

Exposing the 23 Lies & Doctrinal Errors

1. "When the question relative to the sacred festival of Easter..."

   The truth: sacred to pagan traditions, this is a pagan name derived from the goddess Ishtar. (Exodus 20:3, Hosea 2:17)

2. "...arose, it was universally..."

   The truth: Everyone in the universe? Is Constantine the king of the universe? (Isaiah 14:3)

3. "...thought that it would be convenient..."

   The truth: God does not call us to convenience but obedience. (John 15:10)

4. "...that all should keep the feast on one day; for what could be more beautiful and more desirable than to see this festival, through which we receive the hope of immortality, celebrated by all with one accord and in the same manner?...."

   The truth: Without Jews? John 17:21, unity between Jew and Gentile brings the salvation of all mankind. (Psalms 133 and Isaiah 56)

5. "...It was declared to be particularly unworthy..."

   The truth: Yahveh's choice of dates is "unworthy" to Constantine as he sets himself above God's choosing of timings. (Daniel 7:25 and Isaiah 14:13 [Lucifer])

6. "...for this, the holiest of festivals to follow the customs

(the calculation) of the Jews..."

The truth: Which are the original and true calculations? (Leviticus 23:1, Jeremiah 31:31–34)

7. "...who had soiled their hands with the most fearful of crimes, and whose minds were blinded..."

The truth: In John 10:17–18 Yeshua lays His own life down (See also John 3:16.) the accusation that "The Jews killed Christ" has been the incentive for the extermination of millions of Jews from that point onwards and until this day, including the Holocaust. (See Matthew 7:17–20, the fruit of this theology)

8. "...In rejecting their custom..."

The truth: God's custom according to His Word.

9. "...we may transmit to our descendants the legitimate..."

The truth: according to Constantine but not according to the Word of God. (Matthew 26:2, Leviticus 23:1–4, Genesis 1:14, John 20:1–9, Matthew 12:39)

10. "...mode of celebrating Easter which we have observed..."

The truth: pagan name and feast not mentioned in the Holy Scriptures.

11. "We ought not therefore to have anything in common with the Jew, for the Savior has shown us another way"

The truth: Yeshua is Jewish, so if nothing is in common with the Jews, nothing is in common with the Messiah. (Matthew 1, John 19;19, Luke 1:59, Luke 2:21)

12. "our worship following a more legitimate and more

convenient course, the order of the days of the week"

The truth: Constantine legitimizes his own ideas in order to gain political power and control and he attempts to dethrone the Word of God on this subject – setting himself and his opinions above Yah and His unchanging Word.

13. "...And consequently in unanimously..."

The truth: without the Jews from which salvation comes! (John 4:22)

14. "...adopting this mode, we desire, dearest brethren to separate ourselves from the detestable company of the Jew For it is truly shameful for us to hear them boast that without their direction we could not keep this feast. How can they be in the right, they who, after the death of the Savior..."

The truth: Romans 11:15–20 warns the Gentiles not to be arrogant against the Jews or Gentiles will be cut of the Olive tree!

15. "...have no longer been led by reason..."

The truth: True sons of God are not led by reason or Greek philosophy but by the Spirit of God. Since Constantine and the Council of Nicaea, the church in its vast majority has been led by reason and by theologians instead of by powerful apostles. (Romans 8:14, Ephesians 2:20) - these are all Jewish.

16. "but by wild violence, as their delusion may urge them"

The truth: What wild violence is he talking about? Unsupported accusation used many times to incite the masses against the Jews like in the Protocols of the Elders of Zion?

17. "They do not possess the truth in this Easter question, for in their blindness and [15th lie] repugnance to all improvements"

The truth: traditions of demons and men that make null and void the Word of God (Matthew 15:3,4, Mark 7:13)

18. "They frequently celebrate two Passovers in the same year. We could not imitate those who are openly in error. How, then, could we follow these Jews who are most certainly blinded by error?"

The truth: Is following the biblical customs error? Who is really blinded here? Gentiles are supposed to be grafted into Israel's Olive tree and not vice versa! (Romans 11:15–20)

19. "For to celebrate a Passover twice in one year is totally inadmissible."

The truth: 2 Chronicles 30:1–3, it is totally scriptural.

20. "But even if this were not so it would still be your duty not to tarnish your soul by communication with such wicked people (the Jews)."

The truth: In other words, Constantine's purpose is to separate from the Jews and the Torah no matter what! Why? 1 John 4:1–3 states that the spirit of anti-Messiah, in operation through Constantine, removes the identity of Messiah as a Jew, and sets himself above God and His Word and His sovereign choice of choosing the Jews to bring salvation.

21. "You should consider not only that the number of churches in these provinces make a majority"

The truth: God has never worked with "majorities" but with obedience. Trusting in the arm of the flesh or the opinions of men brings about a curse! (Deuteronomy 28:1–14, Jeremiah 17:5, Judges 7:2–8, 1 Samuel 14:6)

22. "...but also that it is right to demand what our reason approves..."

The truth: Human reasoning? (1 Corinthians 1:27, Isaiah 29:14b)

23. "...and that we should have nothing in common with the Jews."

The truth: or with the Jewish Messiah or His salvation – John 4:22, Romans 11:15–20. He set the Gentile part of the church onto a path of self-destruction, remaining a wild olive instead of being grafted into the cultivated Olive tree – which is Israel – because of arrogance, removing the foundations of the Jewish apostles and prophets. (Psalms 11:3, Ephesians 2:20, Revelation 21:14)

Prayer Renouncing the First Council of Nicaea

Please pray. You can copy and pass it on, and please let us

know of your decision.

> Before the Almighty God of Israel, I stand and hereby renounce the First Council of Nicaea as led by Constantine. I renounce its foundation and all the anti-Jewish fruit that came out of it. I renounce every doctrinal error and every lie in it, including replacement theology in all of its aspects.
>
> I hereby affirm my faith in Yahveh, the God of Israel, who is the Creator of the Universe and my Father through the atoning death of His Holy Son Yeshua, who is both the promised Jewish Messiah and God in the flesh. I hereby affirm my faith in the resurrection of Yeshua the Messiah and the outpouring of the Holy Spirit of God from the Day of Shavuot (Pentecost) and onwards, to all that repent and believe in the Son. I hereby affirm my belief that I am grafted into the Olive Tree that represents Israel, and together with the believing Jewish people, I will inherit eternal life. I hereby affirm that the God of Israel will never forsake His people, neither will He forget His covenant with the Jews or with the Ecclesia (Called out Ones - Church).
>
> I thank you, Holy Father, for removing all the curses that have come into my life and into my nation due to our belief in the tenets of faith stated in the Council of Nicaea concerning the Jews and the Jewish

foundations of the faith. I beg you and thank you for pouring out your great mercy and forgiveness over myself, my family, and my nation. I hereby commit myself to walk in truth as You reveal it to me and in love with all my fellow men and especially my (and the Church's) spiritual parents, the Jewish people, according to Genesis 12:1-3.

APPENDIX D
Connect With Us

Other Books

Order now online: www.kad-esh.org/shop/

The MAP Revolution (Free E-Book)
Exposing the Anti-Christ

Defeating Depression
Find Out Why Revival Does Not Come... Yet!

The Identity Theft
The Return of the 1st Century Messiah

From Sickology to a Healthy Logic
The Product of 18 Years Walking Through Psychiatric Hospitals

ATG: Addicts Turning to God
The Biblical Way to Handle Addicts and Addictions

The Healing Power of the Roots
It's a Matter of Life or Death!

Grafted In
It's Time to Take the Nation's!

Sheep Nations
It's Time to Take the Nations!

Restoring the Glory: The Original Way
The Ancient Paths Rediscovered

Yeshua is the Name
The Important Restoration of the Original Hebrew Name of the Messiah

The Bible Cure for Africa and the Nations
The Key to the Restoration of All Africa

The Key of Abraham
The Blessing or the Curse?

Yes!
The Dramatic Salvation of Archbishop Dr. Dominiquae Bierman

Eradicating the Cancer of Religion
Hint: All People Have It

Restoration of Holy Giving
Releasing the True 1,000 Fold Blessing

Vision Negev
The Awesome Restoration of the Sephardic Jews

The Woman Factor by Rabbi Baruch Bierman
Freedom From Womanphobia

The Revival of the Third Day (Free E-Book)
The Return to Yeshua the Jewish Messiah

Music Albums

www.kad-esh.org/shop/

The Key of Abraham

Abba Shebashamayim

Uru

Retorno

Get Equipped & Partner With Us

Global Revival MAP (GRM) Israeli Bible School

Take the most comprehensive video Bible school online that focuses on dismantling replacement theology.
For more information or to order, please contact us:

www.grmbibleschool.com

grm@dominiquaebierman.com

United Nations for Israel Movement

We invite you to join us as a member and partner with $25 a month, which supports the advancing of this End time vision that will bring true unity to the body of the Messiah. We will see the One New Man form, witness the restoration of Israel, and take part in the birthing of SHEEP NATIONS. Today is an exciting time to be serving Him!

www.unitednationsforisrael.org

info@unitednationsforisrael.org

Global Re-Education Initiative (GRI) Against Anti-Semitism

Discover the Jewishness of Jesus and defeat Christian anti-Semitism with this online video course to see revival in your nation!

www.against-antisemitism.com

info@against-antisemitism.com

Join Our Annual Israel Tours

Travel through the Holy Land and watch the Hebrew Holy Scriptures come alive.

www.kad-esh.org/tours-and-events/

To Send Offerings to Support our Work

Your help keeps this mission of restoration going far and wide.

www.kad-esh.org/donations

Contact Us

Archbishop Dr. Dominiquae & Rabbi Baruch Bierman

Kad-Esh MAP Ministries | www.kad-esh.org

info@kad-esh.org

United Nations for Israel | www.unitednationsforisrael.org

info@unitednationsforisrael.org

Zion's Gospel Press | shalom@zionsgospel.com

52 Tuscan Way, Ste 202-412, 32092 St. Augustine Florida, USA

+1-972-301-7087

www.ingramcontent.com/pod-product-compliance
Lightning Source LLC
Chambersburg PA
CBHW021424070526
44577CB00001B/42